ACME BRICK COMPANY

125 YEARS ACROSS THREE CENTURIES

THE
DONNING COMPANY
PUBLISHERS

ACME BRICK COMPANY

125 YEARS ACROSS THREE CENTURIES

by
Bill Beck

The Donning Company Publishers
184 Business Park Drive, Suite 206
Virginia Beach, VA 23462

Lex Cavanah, General Manager
Nathan Stufflebean, Production Supervisor
Richard A. Horwege, Senior Editor
Chad Harper Casey, Graphic Designer
Monika Ebertz, Imaging Artist
Kathy Snowden Railey, Project Research Coordinator
Katie Gardner, Marketing and Production Coordinator

James H. Railey, Project Director

Library of Congress Cataloging-in-Publication Data

Names: Beck, Bill, author.
Title: Acme Brick Company : 125 years across three centuries / by Bill Beck.
Description: Virginia Beach, VA : The Donning Company Publishers, [2016] |
    Includes index.
Identifiers: LCCN 2016017757 | ISBN 9781681840390 (hard cover : alkaline
    paper)
Subjects: LCSH: Acme Brick Company—History. | Acme Brick
    Company—Anniversaries, etc. | Brick trade—Texas—Fort Worth—History. |
    Brickworks—Texas—Fort Worth—History. | Acme Brick Company—Biography. | Fort Worth (Tex.)—Economic conditions.
Classification: LCC HD9605.U64 A363 2016 | DDC 338.7/624183609764—dc23
LC record available at https://lccn.loc.gov/2016017757

Printed in the United States of America at Walsworth

CONTENTS

FOREWORD

Brick have been produced for thousands of years, making them one of the most durable, long-lasting, and sustainable building products that have ever existed. A 125th-year celebration seems just a small step in a journey of many millennia. But, few businesses today have spanned the three different centuries that have marked Acme Brick Company's contribution to the American landscape. In recognition of this remarkable achievement, this book attempts to chronicle the evolution of our company, to highlight its successes, and to visually portray the beauty and permanence that Acme Brick lends to the building of the United States of America.

What differentiates a successful business from one that ultimately fails are its associates. Since its founding in 1891, Acme Brick Company has been blessed with multiple generations of outstanding visionaries, leaders, managers, and workers who have spent their careers creating *Lifetime Customers* by producing, selling, and delivering an extraordinary lineup of building materials. When George Bennett incorporated the Acme Pressed Brick Company, there were literally thousands of brick companies nationwide. Today, approximately sixty remain. When you compare those two figures, it becomes clear that the hardworking men and women of Acme Brick Company have made that one-in-several-thousand difference.

During 2016, Acme Brick Company will produce, sell, and deliver more brick than any other brick producer in the USA for the *ninth* year in a row, a mark that we believe is unprecedented in our industry. It is truly a testament to our founder, George Bennett, who aptly chose the word *Acme*—which Merriam-Webster defines as "the highest point"— for his new brick company 125 years ago.

Enjoy this book. Acme Brick Company and tens of thousands of associates have served an important purpose for many years, we are proud of what has been accomplished, and we are even more excited about what lies ahead!

Sincerely,

Dennis D. Knautz
President & CEO

CHAPTER 1
ACME PRESSED BRICK COMPANY
1891 TO 1916

Since 1891, Texas has been home to one of the most impressive brick manufacturers in the United States. From the outset of its operations, Acme Brick Company (formerly Acme Pressed Brick Company) has succeeded as a result of visionary and aggressive leadership, dedicated and loyal employees, and dependable and reliable products. From its roots in a slowly urbanizing Texas in the late nineteenth century, Acme Brick has contributed to the economic development of the Southwest while becoming the largest American-owned producer of face brick in the world. "For Acme Brick is practically an institution in the Southwest," writes historian and educator Edwin Lehr, "and is known far and wide for its accomplishments, its competitive spirit, its leadership, its stability, its adaptability, and its tenacious desire to be on top."[1] Acme Brick has grown tremendously, despite constant changes in the industry and the country, by remaining flexible and relying on those foundational tenets of aggressive leadership, a dedicated workforce, and superior products. For these reasons, Acme Brick Company has evolved into a titan in the brickmaking industry for the past 125 years.

A History of Foreign and Domestic Brickmaking

Predating the great civilization of the Tigris-Euphrates River Valley, brickmaking is considered one of the oldest industries known to man. The use of bricks in American building came from England, and following the Revolutionary War, domestic production of brick increased as brick became more general in construction. The first U.S. brickmaking patent was issued on May 15, 1800, for "a brick and tile machine invented by G. Hadfield, residence not recorded," according to the Patent Office. Patents increased over the next few decades, with new apparatuses including kilns and dryers being invented throughout the first half of the nineteenth century. After the Civil War, American industry expanded at a tremendous rate, with brickmaking keeping pace with the universal trend toward increased production. In the United States alone, the number of establishments manufacturing clay products jumped from 2,121 in 1850 to 3,959 in 1870.[2]

The Southwest had long been familiar with brick and brickmaking, as adobe and burned brick had been popular among Native Americans, Spanish missions, French colonists

The Acme Pressed Brick Plant near Bennett was situated in a valley between the town of Mineral Wells, Texas, and the Brazos River.

In the days before heavy equipment became commonplace, men with picks and shovels worked at the face of the shale deposit, loading shale into horse-drawn wagons, like here at Bennett in the early twentieth century.

in New Orleans, and Anglo colonists along the Texas Gulf Coast. "It was this undeveloped Texas market that the founder of Acme Pressed Brick Company, George Ellis Bennett, sought to supply in 1891 when he started his face brick business west of Fort Worth," writes Edwin Lehr, an educator for more than four decades and the author of a definitive history of the Texas brick industry.[3]

In the late 1800s, Dallas merchant George Bennett recognized a growing demand for construction materials in the state, as Texans moved out of the frontier stage and cities emerged. With locals demanding substantial lodging other than log cabins, Bennett acknowledged the need for a successful pressed brick factory in the state.[4] Demand for brick in Texas kept pace with the state's general economic development, with the gain in "value of brick produced" growing to about $100,000 a year for the entire decade of the 1880s.[5]

When it comes to producing high-quality and profitable brick, there are several important factors. In addition to

favorable plant facilities, adequate knowledge, and continuing demand, the most vital items needed are: clay or shale, fuel for burning, a favorable labor market, good transportation, and proximity to a growing market area.[6] For two years George Bennett searched for a place where these conditions came together; in 1890 he traveled west of Weatherford in Parker County down the Texas and Pacific Railroad line from Millsap. He arrived at a tributary of the Brazos River called Rock Creek, which cut through a ridge of Pennsylvania Age rock, limestone, and shale that surrounded, in saucer-like fashion, a triangular delta formed by the alluvial deposits of the creek and river.

The intrepid entrepreneur took samples from the soil and creek bank and returned to Dallas, rushing the samples to Chisholm-Boyd-White, a brick machinery company in Chicago, for testing. When the samples came back with a note of being "of good quality and color," Bennett set out to raise the necessary capital for a brickmaking endeavor.

Acme Pressed Brick Company Opens Operations

When George Bennett received news that his samples were of good quality, he immediately began buying up land, purchasing three 160-acre tracts in April 1890 for just over $4 per acre. He then spent months buying machinery, testing samples, attending to legal matters, overseeing plant construction, and taking brick for testing. Construction began on buildings to house the machinery, horses, mules, and tools as well as a blacksmith and repair shop. Roofs were built over the updraft kilns, and houses in the little company town (named Bennett, after its founder) were quickly completed. The brick was perfected using shale from the bank of Rock Creek.

Workers pose outside a large updraft kiln at the Bennett Plant in 1908, the year of the strike.

In the Bennett Plant's updraft kilns, brick were carefully hand-stacked for the most effective firing.

In about 1915, these workers extruded unfired sewer pipe at what is now Acme Brick's Plant near Denver, Colorado.

The updraft kilns had a voracious appetite for fuel, and shoveling coal to feed the kilns required sizable crews of men and mules to accomplish the task.

On March 26, 1891, Bennett produced a marketable brick that was rated "superior." With the new product, the plant went into full production. At that time, the plant "consisted of one two-mold and one three-mold Boyd dry-press brick machine, one 120-horsepower automatic Atlas Engine, two return tubular boilers (52 inches by 14 feet), one 8-foot Frost dry pan, and one 9-foot Frost dry pan for grinding."[7] Pumps, belts, shafting, pulleys, and other tools were also installed.

During these first few months, Bennett also applied for a license to do business in Texas, submitting a statement of expenses to his partners on April 17, 1891, while chartering the Acme Pressed Brick Company at Alton, Illinois. The Acme Pressed Brick charter called for $52,000 worth of capital stock valued at $100 a share, most of which was issued to George Bennett for expenses. Officers were George Bennett, president; George Eaton Root, vice president; and Henry E. Root, secretary and treasurer.

One of the earliest pieces of equipment positioned in the plant was a Boyd Four-Mold Press installed in 1894.

Brickmakers worked hard and lived hard. They often resembled coal miners because of the soot and smoke from the kilns that coated their faces, hands, and clothes.

Above: This Boyd Six-Mold Press installed at the Bennett Plant in the 1890s helped to dramatically increase the efficiency of the production line.

Left: George Bennett brought in experienced brickmen from across the South to staff his new plant.

Manufacturing was a much more intense job in the early days, relying on animal and human muscle. Experienced brickmen were brought in to assist with the early operations, which were extremely busy. Still, through its earliest years, Acme Pressed Brick had more orders than it could fill. The demand forced the company to build four new kilns over the next three years. Business improved so much that Bennett decided to build a new plant across the tracks west of his first plant. This new plant was equipped with a six-mold Boyd Press and a two-mold Boyd Press, bringing the capacity of the brick plants at Bennett Station to seventy-five thousand brick a week. The locations required about three hundred workers to keep operations going.

The original workforce at Bennett was made up of veterans of the brickmaking industry in the South.

As the new century began, Bennett for the first time advertised Acme Pressed Brick Company in a journal for the manufacturers of high-grade pressed brick, common brick, and face and ornamental brick, listing some of the buildings that had been constructed with Acme Brick. These included buildings in nearby Dallas like the McCormick Office Building, Union Depot, Santa Fe Depot, Avery Building, and Maroney Building; churches and factories in Sherman; the Paris Federal Courthouse and Post Office; and the Bowie Courthouse and jail. However, Acme Pressed Brick still had not provided brick for the construction of any major buildings in Fort Worth. The city, which was slowly becoming a meatpacking center in the last decade of the nineteenth century, would soon call on Acme Pressed Brick to rectify that oversight.

On October 7, 1901, Fort Worth citizens raised enough money ($100,600) to assure that Armour and Swift—two of the nation's largest meatpackers—would establish a huge packing plant at the Fort Worth Stockyards, and with it came Acme's first big commercial job. Acme Pressed Brick actually was brought in by Denton Pressed Brick Company, run by well-known local builder William Bryce, who had received the contract. The temporary partnership would develop into a working agreement, with each company helping the other when needed.

Fort Worth's Burk Burnett Building, originally housing the State National Bank, was one of many local buildings constructed of Acme Brick during the early twentieth century.

In the early 1900s, Acme Pressed Brick maintained a company store for workers at the isolated plant.

A steam-powered shovel fills rail cars pulled by mules with shale at the Denton mining pit, circa 1900.

Mines, mills, and plants in the early 1900s prided themselves on the prowess of the company baseball team. Acme Pressed Brick's nine in 1906 included (top row, left to right): Jack Robinson, John A. Elders, Tran Wallace, Jim Lowe, Joe Wallace, and Luther Hatfield, and (seated, left to right): Nathan Lee, George Lee, John Pollard, Doc Elders, and Joe Cox.

The order put Acme Pressed Brick into overdrive. Production at the company had previously totaled 2 million brick per year. Now, the company was required to produce 2 million brick *a month*. As one can imagine, plant capabilities were stretched, with workdays being extended and operations running day and night to keep pace. Work on the meatpacking plant began in January 1902, with the cornerstone being laid three months later. New additions to the successful endeavor kept the plant and company busy through 1910.

Acme Pressed Brick Company's first office was located on the Texas Pacific Railroad tracks in Bennett and was abandoned in 1907.

Economic Panic and a Leader Lost

For the first years of the twentieth century, Acme Pressed Brick Company found itself in the midst of its busiest production schedule since being founded. But that all would change in 1907, as businesses all over the country were affected by one of the worst economic panics in American history. When a 7.8 earthquake hit San Francisco on April 18, 1906, a shockwave was sent through the entire country. "The devastation of that city drew gold out of the world's major money centers," noted Robert F. Bruner, dean of the University of Virginia's Darden Graduate School of Business Administration.[8] Although not necessarily similar to the San Francisco earthquake, the financial contagion caused by Wall Street speculation and excess borrowing created a liquidity crunch that launched a sharp recession starting in June 1907. By October and early November, a full panic had gripped banks in New York City and other American cities, triggered by a failed speculation that caused the bankruptcy of two brokerage firms.[9]

To make matters worse in Texas, Acme Pressed Brick Company was dealing with a tremendous loss of its own in the summer of 1907. On a trip to Galveston

A supervisor at the Bennett Plant, circa 1910; note the book in the pocket of his lab coat.

THE LIFE AND CAREER OF GEORGE BENNETT,
FOUNDER OF THE ACME PRESSED BRICK COMPANY

The story of George Bennett's life and career mirrors that of many other post–Civil War entrepreneurs of his time, during the era that has come to be known as the Gilded Age. Born on October 6, 1852, to Benjamin and Anna Bennett of Springfield, Ohio, George Bennett was one of several children in a typically large nineteenth-century family. George left home at age sixteen and found employment in St. Joseph, Missouri, with a wholesaler named James McCord. After gaining experience in the trade, Bennett did as most aspiring young men would do. He went into merchandizing for himself in Butler, Missouri. But Bennett's business did not survive the post–Civil War depression, and the young businessman lost practically all he owned.

Seeking better fortunes in a new environment, George Bennett moved to Galveston, Texas, later relocating to Dallas, which offered the best opportunity for his trade. The Missouri-Kansas-Texas Railroad had just completed its line to Dallas, adding further occasion for success. Within a year of moving to Dallas, Bennett went to work for the McCormick Reaper and Harvester Company, as opportunities for the sale of farm machinery abounded with the arrival of mechanization and the cash crop system. Bennett held the position of state sales manager for McCormick until 1884, at which time he quit and went into the merchandizing business for himself after making multiple contacts throughout the city. During this time, he also acted as general manager for the Tomkins Implement Company of Dallas until 1890.

While establishing himself and his local merchandizing business, Bennett often traveled to Fort Worth, a town that was bursting with ambition to be the "Queen of the Prairies." On one of his trips in 1882, he met Octavia Hendricks, whose father (Harrison G. Hendricks) had been instrumental in bringing the railroad to Fort Worth. Miss Hendricks and her family were among the old "400" of Fort Worth, meaning that as the young couple's courtship progressed, Bennett and Miss Hendricks attended many of the town's social events. The two were married on September 19, 1884, and their family grew as Bennett and his wife welcomed five children (four daughters and one son) to the world. It was said that Bennett founded Acme Pressed Brick Company in hopes of accumulating something for his young family, which he certainly did.

Beyond his business insight and efforts, George Bennett was an active Mason, having been made a Master Mason in September 1902 at Fort Worth Lodge No. 148. Over the next two years, he took both the York and Scottish Rites. He was a member of the Elks and an enthusiastic supporter of nearly every Fort Worth improvement program.

George Bennett died on July 3, 1907, having left more than successful business ventures to his heirs. "As a businessman, he established a tradition of honest business practices, fair labor policies, high-quality workmanship, lasting friendships, and ethical principles that from its earliest days, gave Acme its enviable reputation. As a leader, his energy and sound decisions set the pace for other Acme executives that came after him. As an entrepreneur, his innovations and imaginative actions gave a character to his company that it still reflects. As a brickmaker, Bennett pioneered new techniques of manufacture, met and beat the market odds and established the first successful face brick company in the Southwest."[1] Because of those reasons and more, Acme Brick Company will always be indebted to their dedicated and visionary founder, George Bennett.

George E. Bennett's 1891 vision created a company that 125 years later has become an institution in U.S. brickmaking.

H. L. Frost came to
the Bennett Plant
from the Denton
Pressed Brick
Company in 1910.

Following the 1910 merger of Acme
Pressed Brick and Denton Pressed Brick,
workers at the two plants sometime
moved back and forth as needed.

H. L. FROST, GEN. MGR.
PHONE 180

Workers gather for a group photo around
and on top of beehive kilns at the Denton
Plant, circa 1907.

Workers at the Denton Plant in 1914 produced pressed brick and fire brick.

in late June, founder and president George Bennett became ill with stomach issues. He died on July 3 in a Galveston hospital and his body was returned to Fort Worth, where he received a Masonic funeral on July 5.

After Bennett's death, his son, twenty-one-year-old Walter R. Bennett, traveled to Alton, Illinois, to attend a stockholder's meeting on August 20, 1907. Despite having grown up at the brickyard, young Bennett was passed over for a steadier and older hand at the helm. Ralph Sellow Root, youngest son of A. K. Root, was elected president, with Walter Bennett becoming vice president and general manager. A well-educated man, Root would remain president from 1907 to 1916. He was not necessarily thrilled with being hurried off to Texas, consequently spending little time at the brick plant and only a half-day at the office. His duties typically consisted of selling brick by telephone and approving customer orders.

As a response to the economic panic, Acme had to take drastic measures. It layed off some workers and curtailed output at its Bennett plant. Angered by the economic depression, layoffs, and wage cuts, plant workers went on strike in 1908, forcing Root and Bennett to close the plant. A long stalemate ensued, though eventually enough young farmers in the area were hired to reopen the Bennett plant in 1909. Irregular production continued throughout 1908–1909, frequently idling the Acme Pressed Brick Company. As a result, the company decided to shut down in the fall of 1910 because of the continuing effect of the 1907 recession.

In blistering Texas summer heat or winter blizzards, workers in the updraft kiln at what is now Bennett Plant meticulously stacked walls of brick for firing.

Reemergence and Expansion at Acme Brick

Things seemed bleak in 1910, as the aftereffects of the Panic of 1907 had caused Acme Pressed Brick Company to close its doors. Luckily for the future of the company, a fortuitous train ride would change all that. One day in December, a Texas Pacific train made an unscheduled stop in Bennett, Texas. The conductor proceeded to inform Ernest Fender that Midland, in West Texas, had been almost completely destroyed by a fire and needed building materials desperately. Fender rushed to Millsap, where he got a banker to lend him enough money for expenses, then caught a fast freight headed west, returning with a tremendous order. That order accomplished two things. It allowed plant superintendent

A. B. Kelly to round up local workers to reopen the plant, and it convinced Walter Bennett to establish a Sales Department, with Fender as its head.

Enough men were hired from the village to reopen the Acme plant. As historian Edwin Lehr writes, the Acme kiln fires "were roaring brightly when Walter Bennett came out to see what had happened. Thoroughly pleased, Bennett placed Fender in charge of sales. For the two men it was the beginning of a lifelong friendship, and for Acme the start of what would become a growing sales organization."[10]

With such a large order and a new focus on sales, Acme Pressed Brick Company was back in business. Its growth allowed the company to move its offices from Millsap to Fort

George Bennett, third from left with the wide-brimmed black hat, visits the Bennett Plant's machine room around the turn of the century.

Worth in 1911. The new offices at 824 Monroe, a one-room affair, housed a staff of four, with a strengthened sales force in Dallas. Soon the one-room office became overcrowded, so headquarters were moved to two rooms on the tenth floor of the First National Bank Building at Seventh and Main in early 1913. Over the next six years, Acme leased every vacated room that became available in the building.

In the midst of these headquarter moves, Acme Pressed Brick Company made its first external expansion. On January 6, 1912, William Bryce (president) and W. E. Guthrie (secretary-treasurer) of Denton Pressed Brick Company signed papers finalizing Acme Pressed Brick's acquisition of Denton Pressed Brick. Acme was recapitalized at $150,000, which required the company to negotiate a loan from Elmo Sledd, a prominent Forth Worth banker, in order to raise the $60,000 in cash needed.

The Denton Plant was located one mile south of Denton's Public Square. William Bryce had organized the Denton Pressed Brick Company in 1901 to develop the rare clay deposits in Denton. Not much changed in operations during the first few years after the merger, with the plant producing 40 million brick from 1912 to 1914. In January 1914, the plant was shut down for extensive repairs, and just when it was finished and "running good," the plant unexpectedly caught fire and burned completely.

W. R. Bennett had received a call from Superintendent A. B. Kelly at six o'clock in the morning about the disaster. Bennett caught a train to Denton, looked at the smoldering ruins, and said "Kelly, we will build this bigger and better than ever."[11] True to his word, the Denton Plant was back into production within sixty days, and by 1918 stiff-mud machinery was installed to complement the dry-press plant. Meanwhile, the Bennett Plant began making updates, with a conversion from dry-press brick

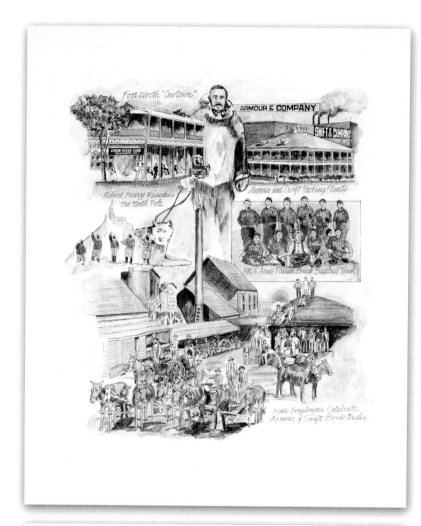

Acme Brick Company memorialized its founding and early years in the 1890s and 1900s during its centennial celebration in 1991.

to stiff-mud operations taking place in 1913. Stiff-mud brick production meant more brick could be made, as it was a continuous operation. It could also produce brick of several shades, textures, shapes, and types.

By 1916, it was clear that Acme Pressed Brick Company would need to undergo a major reorganization. Following the merger with Denton Pressed Brick, ownership had changed and the entire character and operational methods of the company were altered. In March 1916, stockholders called upon Bennett and Bryce to put forth recommendations for the future of the company, which included changing the name of the company. Final approval came from stockholders and directors in Alton on April 13, 1916, changing the name to "Acme Brick Company," and applying for a Texas charter. By May, the name had been changed and a new president had been elected. The stockholders elected twenty-nine-year-old Walter R. Bennett as the first president of newly formed Acme Brick Company, who turned out to be "a greater business genius than his father."[12] With a new name, a reorganized business structure, and innovative new techniques for producing brick, Acme Brick Company was poised to play a critical role in the upcoming boom that accompanied World War I.

The basic flow of materials in the manufacture of brick in a modern plant.
Courtesy of Brick Institute of America.

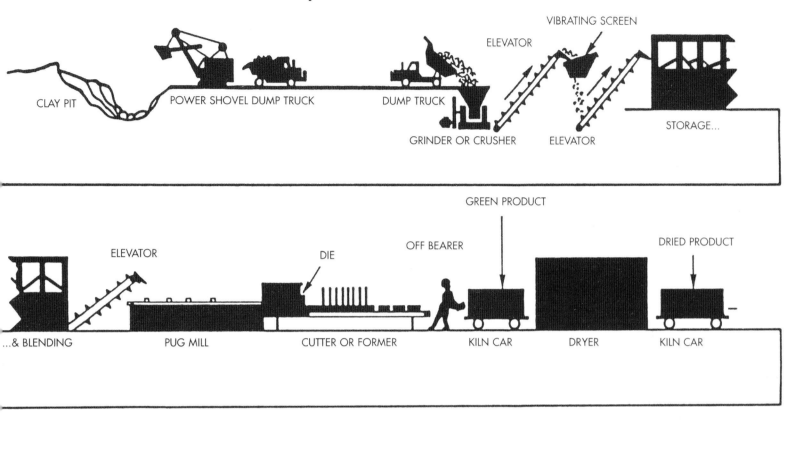

CLAY PIT   POWER SHOVEL DUMP TRUCK   DUMP TRUCK   GRINDER OR CRUSHER   ELEVATOR   VIBRATING SCREEN   ELEVATOR   STORAGE...

ELEVATOR   DIE   OFF BEARER   GREEN PRODUCT   DRIED PRODUCT

...& BLENDING   PUG MILL   CUTTER OR FORMER   KILN CAR   DRYER   KILN CAR

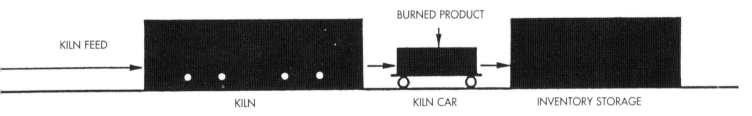

KILN FEED   BURNED PRODUCT

KILN   KILN CAR   INVENTORY STORAGE

Brickmaking has remained remarkably consistent during the past century-and-a-quarter.

CHAPTER 2
FROM BOOM TO BUST

1917 TO 1935

The Denver Plant in the 1920s was located in the foothills some thirty miles south of Denver, Colorado.

When Walter Bennett took the helm of the newly reorganized Acme Brick Company in April 1916 with a sense of boundless energy and determination, the world was in the midst of its first great war. The Southwestern United States anticipated American entry into the war effort, with Texas and other surrounding states experiencing a boom in manufacturing and other industries. Acme Brick was no different, preparing itself for the onset of a global conflict by revamping its Denton plant in time for World War I production. Bennett restructured the finances and organization of his new company while also opening branch sales offices in San Antonio, Houston, and West Texas.

During the late 1910s, Acme Brick and other similar companies certainly felt the effects of the war. It joined the war effort by selling old equipment for scrap, buying large amounts of saving bonds, and making payroll deductions available to employees who wished to use this method to buy war bonds and stamps. The company also supplied brick for many key industries and military bases, such as Camp Bowie.

When the war ended in November 1918, America (and the Southwest specifically) underwent stupendous economic changes. With the popularity of automobile transportation exploding nationwide, the brick business thrived. Muddy streets and roads were replaced with paving brick, the expanded oil industry required additional brick office buildings, and

This Acme Brick Dallas mansion with a carriage house in back was perhaps one of the city's most desirable addresses in the 1920s.

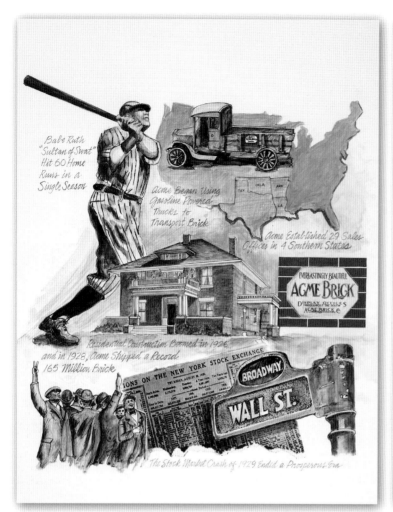

The centennial advertising campaign highlighted Acme Brick in the 1910s and 1920s.

homeowners clamored for more spacious brick quarters. New construction figures between 1919 and 1925 showed a rise of $3.4 billion nationwide, with residential construction in the Southwest representing nearly two-thirds of the total in 1926.[1] Not surprisingly, Acme Brick Company seemed poised for a postwar boom even as early as 1919, selling a record 16 million brick during that year.

For an entire decade, Acme Brick made major changes and expanded into untouched markets. New ventures into new states and new partnerships helped shape its business foundation for decades to come. When the 1920s came to an end, Acme found itself in a relatively strong position to weather the economic depression that would plague the country for nearly the next decade. With great determination and business acumen, Acme found itself standing at the beginning of the next great world war, a testament to its leaders and dedicated workforce.

The growing Dallas middle class in the 1920s proved a ready market for homes like this brick Four Square.

Much of the output at the company's Denver Plant in the 1920s was sewer pipe (foreground) and drain tiles (background).

The Oak Cliff Junction Interurban Station in Dallas was one of the many Acme Brick buildings in the Metroplex in the 1920s.

In the late 1920s, Acme Brick ran a series of advertisements in architectural magazines to highlight the esthetics of brick buildings.

The Roaring Twenties at Acme Brick

When the 1920s began, Acme was poised to grow. The brickmaker's physical operations began to expand into other states beyond Texas in the 1920s. Walter Bennett and Acme's management team spent a great deal of time strategizing and developing plans for everything that accompanied this growth, particularly paying attention to the sales organization (which had to be reorganized into five divisions during this time).

With sales offices opening all over the Southwest during the 1920s, Acme Brick also looked to improve its advertising and public relations as part of its overall sales strategy. The company advertised in professional, architectural, and clay products journals as well as *The Pug Mill*, the company house organ that was distributed to architects, contractors, and other major customers (as well as Acme Brick employees). Company slogans were initiated during this time, such as: "Acme Brick— Everlastingly Beautiful"; "Brick—the Noblest of Building Materials"; "A Well-Burned Clay Never Decays—Specify Acme Brick"; "Face Brick Walls Require No Upkeep"; "A Brick for

The company newsletter, *The Pug Mill*, advertised the rich color of Acme Brick in 1927.

The ornate brickwork of the Adolphus Hotel in Dallas has delighted travelers to Dallas for more than a century.

One of the most important things built at the Perla Plant was the railroad siding.

Every Type—A Color for Every Color Scheme"; "There is No Substitute for Brick"; and "Build Insurance into Your Homes with Fire-resistive Burned-Clay Products." These slogans spread Acme Brick's name throughout the Southwest and burnished the company's reputation as Acme Brick began expanding into new locations in Texas and beyond.

As a result of record sales in 1919, Walter Bennett began planning and reviewing potential sites for Acme's first plant outside of Texas. He looked to Arkansas in 1919 and 1920, to the small lumber and clay product town of Malvern, located twenty-five miles south of Hot Springs. His interest in this area led him to purchase a 120-acre half-wilderness and half-cotton patch tract near Perla, Arkansas, in 1920 for $500 an acre.

A crew at the Bennett Plant in the early 1920s.

A company brick plant crew poses on brick platform, circa 1930s.

Construction of a new brick plant began in the spring of 1920 and was completed by October 1921.

Upon the completion of the Perla Plant, Walter Bennett predicted that the plant would produce 1 million brick per month initially and would eventually reach a total output of 2 million brick a month. That number proved significantly low, as the Perla Plant would go on to produce more than 3 million face brick *a week* in the spring of 1971. But as of November 1921, the Perla Plant had received only a few orders. So when it was asked by Fort Smith Brick Company to produce seventeen thousand Acme Ruffs, the words on the order prophetically announced "We're off."[2] The face brick business continued to boom throughout the 1920s, and Acme's Perla crew was particularly busy by mid-decade. The employees developed new and unique blends while loading cars of brick between twelve and fourteen hours a day.

The Oklahoma City Plant takes delivery of a brand-new fleet of tandem vehicles in 1924.

The Tip of the Expansion Iceberg

The new Perla Plant was only the tip of Acme's expansion iceberg during the decade. In response to other companies trying to move in and go into business in Malvern, Bennett began negotiating with Fort Smith Brick and Tile Company and Arkansas Brick and Tile Company even prior to the completion of the first Perla Plant. On April 13, 1923, the Fort Smith Brick Company agreed to a merger with Acme Brick, which was the first out-of-state acquisition made by the company. The merger was based on a small amount of cash and a significant increase in stock. According to a history of Acme Brick Company, the April 1923 Stockholders' Meeting has been considered one of the most important in the history of the company, with fourteen people and fourteen proxies representing 85 percent of the shares deciding to absorb Fort Smith Brick Company by recapitalization. Acme Brick paid $125,000 for the company in the form of 1,250 shares of the new common stock while also paying a dividend of 2,000 shares ($100 par value) to its stockholders.

Fort Smith, located on the Arkansas and Oklahoma state line about 165 miles northwest of Little Rock and 305 miles northeast of Fort Worth, was a major hub for rail transportation. The convergence of six rail lines made Fort Smith a burgeoning industrial metropolis in the early 1900s. The Fort Smith Brick Company was organized when seventy miles of street needed bricks for paving. With the 1923 merger, Acme Brick added two

plants, one at Fort Smith and the other at Mansfield, Arkansas. The Mansfield Plant was to be shut down, while the Fort Smith Plant (then the largest paving brick plant in the South) was converted to face brick operations. Fort Smith's "Heritage Brick" of mixed textures, irregular shapes, and otherwise defaced brick soon became a "bestseller."[3]

The company's animal barn northeast of the Bennett Plant was in use until the mid-1920s, when Acme Brick abandoned the use of mules at the Texas plant.

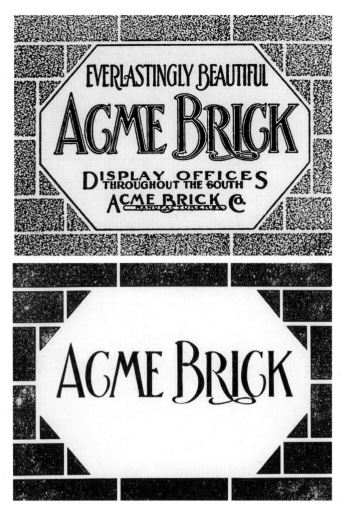

Two Acme Brick logos from the 1920s.

The following year, the opportunity arose for Acme Brick to move up the Arkansas River when it acquired Oklahoma-based American Brick and Tile Company in 1924 for about $300,000. American Brick and Tile had been organized in 1901 and had its home office in Oklahoma City, Oklahoma.[4] It had acquired the Cleveland Brick Company of Cleveland, Oklahoma, in 1919

and steadily made inroads into North Texas, Kansas, Arkansas, and even into West Tennessee in the 1920s.

By the mid-1920s, Cleveland was a thriving town located on the Missouri-Kansas-Texas (M-K-T, "the Katy") Railway and the Arkansas River. The Cleveland Plant was located less than two miles northwest of town on the M-K-T Railway. However, its operations were anything but modern when Acme Brick purchased it in 1924, manufacturing only building tile during the 1920s and early 1930s. The Oklahoma City Plant, on the other hand, produced a greater variety of products and had a greater potential. It produced about one hundred thousand brick per day, consisting of approximately forty thousand dry-press and sixty thousand stiff-mud brick. Still, the purchase of American Brick and Tile would not be Acme Brick's last foray into Oklahoma.

While negotiating the purchase of American Brick and Tile, Acme Brick began to construct an entirely new facility at Tulsa, Oklahoma (the "oil capital of the world"), which helped expand the company's stronghold into a third state in 1925. Tulsa was a burgeoning city, having grown its population from a few thousand in 1910 to more than 120,000 in 1926.[5]

Acme Brick's Tulsa Plant was built four miles east of the city, on the St. Louis and San Francisco Railway, within the switching limits of three other railroads. Its site was purchased in 1925 for the construction of a "most modern brick plant," according to plans.[6] Construction began in November 1925 and was completed the following summer. The Tulsa Plant was particularly modern, and many knew it for its unique pit. The pit and plant site adjoined a coalmine, so shale that had been removed to get at the coal was used for brickmaking. The shale was twenty to twenty-five feet thick. Acme attained the right burn for the Tulsa brick material in its eighteen-chambered Hoffman Continuous Kiln and its four downdraft kilns, manufacturing twenty-five thousand common brick and twenty thousand face brick per day.

A typical plant layout in the 1920s showing round kilns to the left and the importance of a rail siding in the foreground.

Workers assembling a shale planer in the World War I era.

Workers making White Perla Brick, circa 1931.

Strategic Partnerships

While Acme Brick built new plants and acquired new companies, it also had the foresight to enter into new strategic partnerships with other companies that would benefit both entities for decades to come. One such partnership was with Elgin-Standard Brick Company of Elgin, Texas. The partnership began in 1918 when both Elgin and Acme Brick bid for the same job in Amarillo, Texas. Ernest Fender tried to sell Acme Brick's Denton product, and the buyer found himself torn between Acme Brick's impressive reputation and the lighter-colored Elgin product. Over a nickel beer, G. W. Prewitt (owner and salesman for Elgin) discussed the matter with Fender, with both men recognizing that Fender could make the sale if he sold a lighter-colored brick. Prewitt ultimately allowed Fender to offer the Elgin product under the Acme Brick name, leading to Fender closing the sale.

The profitable agreement that followed, and which was finalized with a handshake, involved each company brokering the other's products in the future. During the 1920s, the tie between the two companies was so close that Acme Brick could run an article in its magazine about "The Elgin Plant" and it would be met with no disapproval. The handshake and "nickel beer agreement" lasted for over fifty years when, in 1964, Prewitt's son, J. K. "Buddy" Prewitt, sold the business to Butler Brick Company, also of Elgin, Texas.[7]

Enlarging the Arkansas Operations

In the second half of the 1920s, Acme Brick Company continued to enlarge its Arkansas operations as the availability of greater financial resources made possible the establishment of more plants outside of Texas. For some time Walter Bennett had been interested in developing a lighter-colored brick and explored Arkansas for a possible production site to do that.[8] In 1926, Acme Brick Company purchased the Arkansas Brick and Tile Company for $600,000, agreeing to pay $300,000 in cash as well as to assume Arkansas Brick and Tile debts amounting to $300,000. By April 1926, all the cash notes had been paid off.

A panoramic view of the Bennett Plant in 1933 showing how many brick were in inventory during the Great Depression.

The purchase of Arkansas Brick and Tile was considered by many to be a "masterstroke," as it gave Acme Brick the competitive edge over brick imported from St. Louis, Missouri.[9] With the acquisition, the company added Arkansas plants in Malvern, Pine Bluff, and Little Rock. The Malvern Plant was particularly successful, as it was already producing in 1926 when Acme Brick acquired it. Bennett had been looking at the plant for years, even buying the land near the plant from Malvern Lumber Company in 1921–1922. However, the plant struggled to significantly improve for several decades, partly due to geographical and equipment troubles.

Part of the Arkansas Brick and Tile purchase included the old Atchison Brick Works, which would become the second plant at Perla. The plant required extensive repairs, with Acme Brick having to remodel the dryer and add a new machine room, grinding room, dry pass, and a clay shed. A Bonnot brick machine was moved from Denton to the new plant, and the second Perla Plant was soon converted to production of building and face tile. Perla No. 1 also received upgrades during this time. A tunnel kiln, which was a new innovation that would increase production, was installed in 1929 while business was still good. Four hundred feet long, gas-fired, with the capacity of fifty-nine cars, Kiln "A" burned 2,223 brick per hour.

In 1927, with its Pine Bluff Plant failing to prove profitable, Acme acquired Wichita Falls Brick and Tile Company in Wichita Falls, Texas. This large plant, having operated for more than a decade

in that area, had a good market for its products. While Acme had the plant initially make both dry-press and stiff-mud brick, within a few years it stopped the dry-press method. The Wichita Falls Plant operated well for a few years, with a capacity of about 20 million brick a year.[10] Unfortunately, by the early 1930s those impressive numbers would be drastically reduced, as the country plummeted into the worst economic slowdown of the twentieth century.

The Great Depression Hits Acme Brick

The acquisition of Wichita Falls Brick and Tile Company marked the end of Acme's period of considerable expansion. In 1927, Acme employed approximately nine hundred employees who shipped 140 million brick. The next year in 1928, Acme sold more than 165 million brick, a total that went unsurpassed for twenty years. The company had experienced two more years of outstanding production and sales, with storage yards nearly cleaned out despite an attempt to keep 2 million brick in reserve stock. Acme was similarly optimistic in 1929, with the company shipping 155 million brick. By 1929, Acme Brick had the capacity to make 170 million face brick a year in its eleven plants scattered across the Southwest, but year after year its capacity was taxed. During this peak, the company's net worth was $3,666,970, almost ten times pre–World War I assets totaling $386,129.58 in 1917.

By the end of the 1920s, Acme had experienced as profitable and successful a decade as it could have hoped for in the wake of World War I. In ten years, the company's physical operations had

Duran Stubblefield was Acme Brick's top salesman in the 1920s and 1930s.

White Perla Brick was used in the construction of this Texas gas station in the 1930s.

expanded as it purchased four other brick companies with their nine plants, modernized its two original Texas plants, built two additional plants (Perla No. 1 and Tulsa), and formed a mutually beneficial alliance with Elgin-Standard. It redesigned its financial structure and established sound operating procedures while also strategically placing service outlets and sales offices throughout the Southwest and the nation. Twice before 1930, Acme Brick

stock was recapitalized, bringing it from $150,000 to $600,000. As its centennial history noted, "Acme Brick Company entered the [1930s] as a large, modern, efficient, and prominent clay products enterprise" that had weathered many challenges; still, the stock market crash of October 1929 and the subsequent Depression rocked Acme Brick (and all other similarly-large companies) to the core, affecting its prosperity for years.

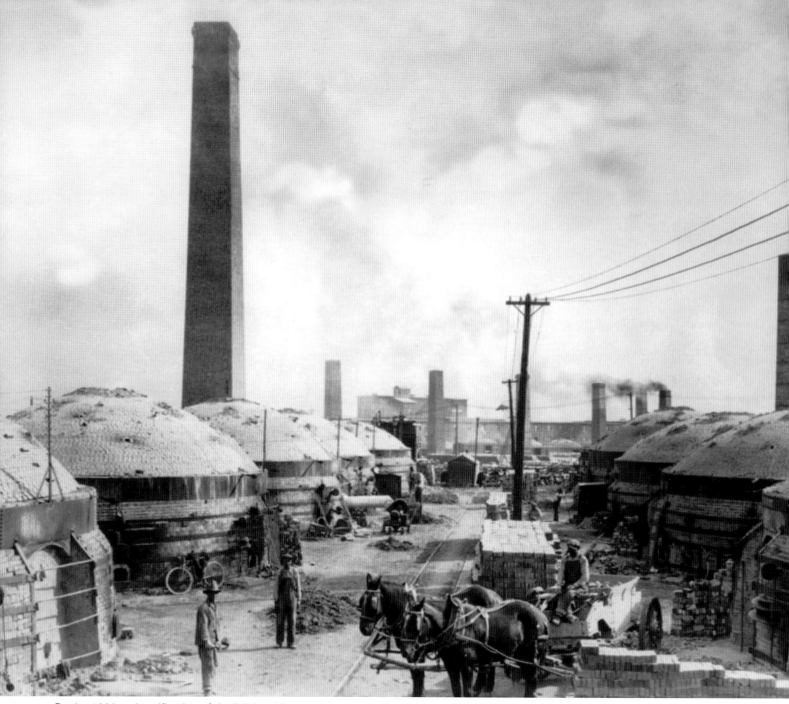

By the 1920s, electrification of the brickmaking process was well under way at the company's Denver Plant.

Drastic Declines In Sales

The Great Depression was devastating for all corners of the country, and states like Texas, Arkansas, and Oklahoma were no exception. At Acme Brick Company, the Depression meant drastic declines in sales and ever-increasing stacks of brick in the yards. In 1930, sales plummeted 40 percent to 98 million brick. The company was forced to close several plants, including the Pine Bluff Plant (which produced bricks of soft-mud, hand molded from poor-grade surface clays, and burned in five updraft kilns) in 1929. Despite its excellent location and core of willing and skilled workers, the Little Rock Plant only lasted a year longer than Pine Bluff, closing in 1930 (although it was later reopened following World War II). The Little Rock operation, which was physically the largest plant in the Acme Brick system, only produced common brick and building tile, both of which were losing popularity in the market. Finally, Acme Brick was forced to close the Wichita Falls Plant, which had produced well for the company following its acquisition in the late 1920s.

The Great Depression greatly affected operations for years at Acme Brick. Labor strife and shrinking markets forced the company to bring multiple plant operations to an end.[11] Acme Brick was forced to close sixteen of its twenty-eight sales offices in a two-year span. Despite wage cuts and temporary schedules,

THE LIFE AND CAREER OF WALTER BENNETT,
SECOND GENERATION TO HEAD ACME BRICK COMPANY

Walter Bennett remains one of the most important presidents in the history of Acme Brick Company. He took over the company when he was twenty-nine, though at the time he had ten years of executive experience in the brick business. Described as "quiet," "even-tempered," and "energetic," Walter Bennett's demeanor and training marked him as a potential leader for the company.

As a child, Walter Bennett would go with his father and Acme founder, George Bennett, to the brick plant. He worked every task at the plant as he got older before his father sent him on an incredible world tour when he was fifteen. He first traveled to the Far East where he worked for an uncle who was an engineer and explorer. After a year in Siam, he went to Europe in 1902, and visited India, the Near East, the Mediterranean, and Latin countries en route to England. The brick Bennett gathered on his international trips would become the foundation for the company's twenty-first-century museum at its Fort Worth headquarters. When Bennett returned to the States, he began working for his father. He rose to the position of vice president and general manager of Acme Pressed Brick Company.

As president of Acme Brick, Walter Bennett worked to improve the Acme brand as best he could. He made tremendous strides in producing brick of remarkable colors, blends, texture, strength, durability, and overall beauty. "Under his open-minded leadership, dozens of new types of brick and tile were developed and patented," noted a history of Acme. "Bennett borrowed ideas from wherever he could and encouraged his employees in both sales and production to do the same."[1] He oversaw particularly momentous times at Acme Brick, and to a large degree the company's success must be attributed to the strong company spirit, enthusiasm, pride, and cooperative desire that Bennett developed in his workforce. As he once memorably put it, "I make my living from people's prosperity; not their troubles like many other professionals."[2]

Bennett also enjoyed the companionship of a dedicated wife, Ethel Evarts, who became an active member of Acme's Board of Directors seven years after her husband's death. Together they had three children: two girls, Lena and Ethyl, and one son, Walter. He was involved in many civic enterprises, from being the first chairman of the Tarrant County Water Development Board (which helped improve water resources, such as the Eagle Mountain Lake) to being an active member of Fort Worth Club, River Crest Country Club, Royal Arch, Knight's Templar Masons and Shrine, and a member of the Board of Directors for both the Texas and Pacific Railroad and the Fort Worth Chamber of Commerce.

sales plunged to 24 million brick in 1932 from about 100 million brick in 1930. At Denton alone, more than 12 million brick were stacked up awaiting shipping orders that never seemed to come. Assets dwindled from more than $4,200,000 to just over $2,000,000 in 1933. The company was recapitalized downward for the only time in its history.

Bennett and company officials tried their best to keep Acme Brick from collapsing, and they actually succeeded. Acme Brick continued to pay its bills, reduced its debt, invested in federal securities, and ultimately fared better than many other brick companies nationwide. Despite the best efforts of the management team, however, Acme Brick Company still experienced some of its worst years financially in 1933 and 1934. In 1934, the worst year of the Depression, Acme Brick recorded its first loss in its storied history, going $120,632 into the red as a result of sales slipping to 20 million brick.

The Depression years were not entirely negative for Acme Brick, especially when it involved its ally, the

The Denver Sewer Pipe & Clay Company lined up all of its trucks for a summer parade in 1935.

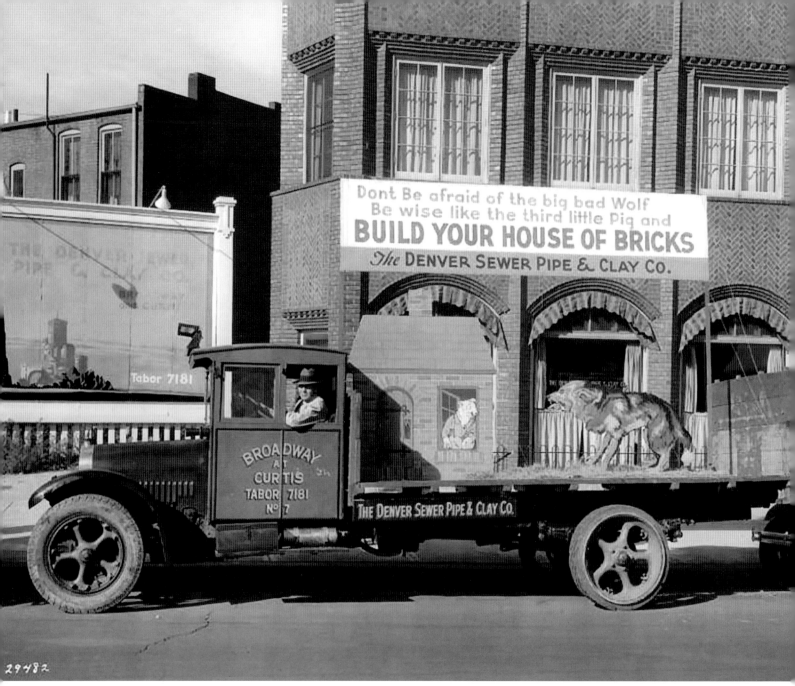

The Denver Sewer Pipe & Clay Company, now part of Acme Brick, sponsors a 1934 parade float showing the wise little pig who built his house of brick.

Bridgeport Brick Company, against out-of-state competition. Forced into bankruptcy in 1930, Bridgeport was aided by Acme Brick in the early years of the Depression. When it could not stave off the courts any longer, Bridgeport Brick Company was delivered into receivership. In 1934, Acme Brick took up the debts of most of its plants (Ferris, Bridgeport, and Mexia, Texas) but left other affiliates to be sold to creditors. By the following year, Bridgeport Brick had resumed production, with Ferris following shortly after. With the nation pinning its hopes of recovery on President Franklin D. Roosevelt's New Deal programs, Acme Brick Company seemed poised to rebound from economic calamity.

The Great Depression Takes a Leader

While Acme Brick finally began to make its way out of the Great Depression, its president would unfortunately suffer a different fate. Distressed by the cares of the company during the Depression, and "crushed by the burdens of responsibility thrust upon," Walter Bennett began to fall into poorer and poorer health. His weight dropped, and the once-energetic and robust leader found himself running the business by telephone and conferences in a hospital bed for months in the winter of 1934–1935. Bennett died on January 15, 1935, at which time "Acme suffered its greatest loss of the depression."[12]

Without Walter Bennett, Acme turned to Bennett's longtime friend and business associate, Senior Vice President

William Bryce, to fill the void in the company. Bryce was born in Scotland, the son of a masonry contractor, and immigrated to Canada in 1869 at the age of eight. He went to Winnipeg, Manitoba, at the age of nineteen to learn bricklaying. He came to the United States in 1881, settling in Fort Worth in 1883. A journeyman bricklayer, he eventually went into business for himself and built his business into one of the largest building firms in Texas and the South. He entered the real estate business, forming the Bryce Building Company in the 1890s and constructing many notable structures in Fort Worth before entering politics and becoming mayor of the city from 1927 to 1933. He was an adviser to Acme and a friend to Bennett for many years.

After Walter Bennett's death, William Bryce immediately assumed the legal duties of president and board chairman. At the same time, Acme Brick also set up a new administrative structure in order for the company to operate effectively. This new structure called for a president of the Board of Directors,

The brick Daniels & Fisher Tower dominated the Denver skyline in the 1920s and 1930s.

who would also be president of Acme Brick Company, and a senior vice president and general manager, who would actually run the company. This would prove critical, as Bryce would only remain president and Board chairman until 1941, at which time another legendary Acme executive would take the helm as president.

CHAPTER 3
WAR AND THE RETURN OF PROSPERITY

1936 TO 1959

From the mid-1930s through the end of the 1950s, Acme Brick Company experienced fifteen of the most exciting years in company history. Having survived the Great Depression, the company looked to a new period of prosperity and financial stability. With the onset of a second world war in a generation, Acme Brick once again joined the war effort and strategically planned for American life once the hostilities ceased. After the war, Acme Brick expanded its reach into new areas, and the company added new leadership that would help guide Acme through an exciting period of expansion and growth. By 1960, Acme Brick found itself poised to meet every new challenge and opportunity it faced in both the Southwestern brick industry and the national economy as a whole.

A Volatile Time

For Acme Brick and other manufacturing companies around the United States, the 1930s were a volatile time. Those who survived the worst years of the Great Depression did so through sacrifice, strategic planning, and a modicum of luck. Acme Brick improved its chances of recovering from the effects of the Great Depression by also utilizing New Deal programs like the National Recovery Administration's short-lived "Blue Eagle" program, which helped the industry and led to the strong union movement of the era, making labor a partner with business.[1] This helped Acme Brick reopen its Bridgeport and Ferris Plants in 1935.

Brick makes its way down the production line at a company plant in the mid-1930s.

The Perla Plant in the late 1940s; the building in the foreground is the plant's natural gas terminal station.

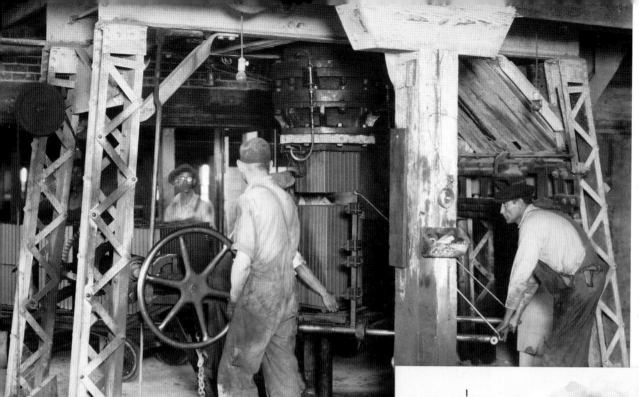

Workers extruding clay structural tile at the Denver Plant in the 1930s.

At its 1991 centennial, Acme Brick looked back on the 1930s, 1940s, and 1950s.

Acme Brick employees, circa 1938; a few are enjoying a beer.

The brick Merchants Biscuit Company in Denver, circa the late 1930s.

The Depression affected various Acme Brick plants differently. For instance, the Bennett Plant nearly stopped production in 1933, although men still stayed on the payroll and performed maintenance tasks. In contrast, operations at Perla and Denton were halted in the early 1930s. The Tulsa Plant operated at near full production after 1936 except for 1938 and 1940, which coincided with down years for Fort Smith and Oklahoma City. The Wichita Falls Plant had its lowest production and profit record in 1936–1937, while Malvern closed down completely in 1933.

Acme Brick took other measures to recover from the Depression. It expanded the Refractories

that was to serve the company during the next two decades of tremendous growth. The Board abolished the position of vice president and general manager, instead creating a chairman of the Board. Under this new system, William Bryce became chairman of the Board and James Ernest Fender assumed the responsibilities and title of president of Acme Brick Company, a position he held until 1959.[2]

For the next few years, more and more responsibility devolved upon the company's vice presidents and managers. By 1946, the lines of authority had become more formalized and clearly defined. Fender, the president and general manager, relied heavily on subordinate managers who acted in the capacity of vice presidents. "This manager–vice president concept had evolved out of Fender's long experience in sales with Acme Brick Company."[3] With his sales background, it was not surprising that gross sales rose to more than $2 million by the early 1940s under Fender's leadership, though net worth did not rise as much (due to debt reduction and large outlays in dividends). Still, as war intensified abroad, Acme's sales in 1942 surpassed the 100 million brick mark for the first time since 1929. It was a sign that economic hardship was finally far behind.

A shale planer in action at Fort Smith, Arkansas, in 1946.

A print logo used in the 1930s and into the 1940s.

Department, sought less and less residential business, and turned to institutional (both industrial and commercial) markets. The brickmaker had to deal with labor issues, which included the unionization of the Malvern, Perla, and Bridgeport Plants in the 1930s and workers at Bridgeport striking in the 1940s. Acme Brick was not antilabor but antiunion, as its leaders and management team had always supported its workers with better-than-average wages and treatment. Finally, around 1935, Acme Brick tried to revive its Sales Department, attempting to reacquire sales territory lost during the Depression. While all these efforts helped Acme Brick survive economic downturn of the 1930s, it was the election of a new president that finally solidified the company's position as the 1940s began.

At the 1941 Stockholders' Annual Meeting, the temporary leadership structure established in 1935 was replaced by one

Acme Brick During World War II

The outbreak of any war inherently brings with it an upsurge in sales and production for manufacturing. When war broke out in Europe in September 1939, Acme Brick experienced that brief increase in sales, although orders fell off again during the period of the "phony war" in the fall of 1939 and winter of 1940. When Nazi Germany began its blitzkrieg attacks against France in the spring of 1940, America's industrial output once again surged, and Acme Brick's refractory business began to go into high gear.[4] Production reached 1925 levels, and by 1941, when German armies invaded Soviet Russia, Acme Brick had sold 85 million bricks, the largest amount in more than a decade. While stockholder confidence was restored and sales were reviving, the company still ran at only half capacity.[5] Acme Brick quickly ramped up production, however, to provide brick for the defense

A pug mill extrudes clay tile at the Denver Plant, circa 1940s.

Supervisors stand on twisted girders and survey the damage after the fire at Perla on December 11, 1944.

industry in Texas and the Southwest following the December 1941 attack by Imperial Japan on the U.S. Naval Base at Pearl Harbor. During the war, the growing refractories business and tile manufacturing accounted for the greater part of production, while face brick sales surged briefly after Pearl Harbor. In 1943, the government set priorities for building materials, allowing few face bricks to be sold or produced.[6]

Students learn about how women helped the government and private companies during World War II to fill the gap in labor left by all those men who went to fight on the front lines. At Acme Brick, women were hired to handle, truck, and off-bear brick, as well as to do clerical work formerly done by men. However, unbeknownst to many, German and Italian prisoners of war were also employed at many domestic manufacturing firms, especially after late 1942. At Acme Brick, German POWs helped produce the badly needed clay products that went into industrial furnaces, war plants, and military construction from 1943 to 1945. In late 1943, POWs from the European and North African Campaign were brought in and put to work in many Acme Brick Plants, including Perla, Fort Smith, Bennett, Denton, Bridgeport, and Oklahoma City.[7]

An aerial view of the Garrison Plant in 1946, one of the company's facilities that utilized German prisoners of war during World War II.

Masons repairing a kiln in the 1940s.

Overall, the POW record was spotty. Some of the prisoners were good workers at some company plants while others were poor workers at other plants. There was only one known escape attempt, and some POWs did get hurt during production. However, many of these men worked hard, and at the Garrison Plant, a plaque was placed on one of the kilns commemorating the fact that it was constructed by prisoners of war.

Late in the war, Acme began to convert from defense to civilian production. It looked toward postwar production and expansion by acquiring its first plant in ten years. The 1944 purchase of the Clinton, Oklahoma Plant from Ray Corner (who owned the Western Brick Company) was part of Acme Brick's strategy as it emerged from the war: to meet the anticipated boom in housing and construction materials after the war.

Postwar Expansion

The Clinton purchase would not be the last acquisition completed by Acme in the postwar years of the late 1940s. In fact, the company followed up the Clinton purchase with two acquisitions in 1945: the Bishop Brick Company and the Garrison Vitrified Brick Company of Garrison, Texas. The Bishop Brick Company, purchased in September 1945, included a Houston Plant built in 1935 that formerly belonged to Ferris Brick Company. The location was originally a dry-press plant, though Acme Brick soon installed stiff-mud machinery and experimented with stiff-mud tile there. The Garrison Vitrified Brick Company dated back to 1893, and its plant belonged to Athens Brick and Tile. After Acme Brick purchased the plant in 1945, it modernized the facility in the 1950s with a new clay shed, grinding rooms, machine room, and an additional kiln.

Following World War II, Acme Brick heavily promoted the building of ceramic homes, seen here at two homebuilding sites in Austin in 1949.

Workers and their families at the Bennett Plant employee picnic in 1949 enjoyed barbecue and gospel music.

This postwar aerial view of the Perla Brick Plant with tunnel kiln and beehive kilns indicates that brickmaking had changed little since early in the twentieth century.

The Bennett Plant crew in March 1951; many had returned to the plant from wartime service.

In the summer of 1950, the country once again found itself preparing for war. The United States' entry into the Korean War following North Korea's invasion of South Korea again brought a fear of shortages, stimulating the brick business and illustrating the cyclical effects that war can have on the industrial economy. Refractories increased output, face brick sales fell off, and existing housing shortages accentuated the trend (much like World War II), with an amplified fall and then rise in building materials needs. Again looking ahead, Acme Brick tried to take advantage of the market demands through a lease purchase arrangement, buying plants at Monroe and Baton Rouge, Louisiana.

Acme Brick purchased the Monroe plant from the Frizzell Brick Company, though the plant was at first operated on a lease agreement pending the settlement of the Frizzell estate. The Baton Rouge Plant, on the other hand, was twice as valuable as the Monroe Plant. The plant had used several outdated kilns

Above: White Brick emerging from a kiln at the Perla Plant in 1949.

Left: Walter Bennett, Jr., second from right, front row, was one of Fort Worth's business leaders in the 1930s and 1940s.

Above: A worker pours a mold from a one-hundred-pound sack of refractory concrete sometime in the early 1950s.

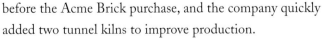

Right: Workers packaging brick from a beehive kiln at the Denver Plant in the 1950s.

before the Acme Brick purchase, and the company quickly added two tunnel kilns to improve production.

Looking at Acme Brick Company's financial situation by the early 1950s, it was clear that the economic environment had improved and the strategic decisions made by Acme's leadership team had paid off. The company's book value had increased from $50 to nearly $80 a share. The huge demand for brick in the late 1940s meant that sales skyrocketed, with annual revenue tripling from $3 million to $9 million between 1945 and 1950. This

meant that an increased sales force was needed in addition to more plants to meet postwar demands.

All these improvements and expansions also required a new headquarters for the company. By 1951, Acme Brick had outgrown its office space in the Neil P. Anderson Building and had begun construction of new office headquarters on West Seventh Street in downtown Fort Worth. The unique four-story structure was completed in October 1952. Windowless, except for four decorative windows and a glassed-in front lobby because of fire codes, the new

Neil P. Anderson Building on Seventh Street in Fort Worth served as Acme Brick's Headquarters throughout most of the 1940s and into the early 1950s; the company's office was on the third floor.

The Acme Brick logo on the elevator doors in the brick lobby of the new headquarters in 1952.

Acme Brick's newly completed Fort Worth Headquarters on Seventh Street in 1952.

THE LIFE AND CAREER OF JAMES ERNEST FENDER

James Ernest Fender, the company's fifth president, was a longtime official who took over as senior vice president and general manager when Walter Bennett passed away. Like many Acme associates, James E. Fender had a long career. He directed company affairs with great skill. When he took over as president in 1941, Fender was the oldest executive from point of service in the Acme Brick organization, having started with the company in 1907.

Born in Terrell, Texas, on January 17, 1883, James was one of five children. He had three sisters and a brother. In1887, the Fender family moved to Fort Worth. The following year, Ernest's father, a lumberman, was tragically killed in a railroad accident. Fender finished high school around the turn of the new century, after which he went to work for Nash Hardware Company (where he had worked during summers in high school). While serving as a bill collector, he attended old Fort Worth University where he was active in the men's choral group, the Arions.

In 1903, Fender decided to seek his fortune in California. After a short while in the Golden State, he journeyed to Seattle, Washington, where he went to work as a laborer for the Renton-Holmes Lumber Company. Fender rose from laborer to clerk to buyer and finally to salesman, which required him to travel at home and abroad. While waiting to board a ship for Hamburg, Germany, in 1906, he received news that his mother had fallen ill. Faced with a difficult decision between family and work, Fender gave his termination notice to Renton-Holmes and returned to Fort Worth. He sought employment as he stayed by his mother's side, watching as she gradually improved.

While back in Texas, Fender was introduced to Walter Bennett by his friend, Eddie Newell. Bennett and Fender had known each other in high school and complemented each other well, Bennett the businessman and thinker and Fender the extrovert salesman. So on January 5, 1907, Fender began as a timekeeper and bookkeeper at Acme Brick's Company Store. For the next thirty years, the history of Acme Brick revolved around these young men and their efforts to build the company. Bennett managed the company as vice president while Fender worked as timekeeper, bookkeeper, salesman, and shipping clerk. Fender became secretary of Acme Pressed Brick when it merged with Denton Pressed Brick, and he later rose to the position of vice president and general sales manager, as well as secretary of the Board of Directors, when Acme Brick was rechartered.

Fender married Katilee Martin of Weatherford in 1913, with whom he had two sons, Howard Martin and James Ernest. Fender shaped the expanding Sales Department during the 1920s, and as senior vice president and general manager he ran the company during the last half of the 1930s before his promotion to president in 1941.[1] Even as early as 1939, he had a well-oiled machine in place at the company, with procedures for sales, production, and office operations all worked out.

It has also been noted that Fender himself "set the example for his staff by becoming vigorously involved in affairs outside the company and urging his officers to do the same."[2] He was active in Rotary and Masonic affairs, served on the Board of Directors of the National Manufacturers Association, and acted as president of the Texas Manufacturers Association, board member of Trinity University, trustee of the First Presbyterian Church, board member of the Belt Line Railway Company, and member of the Trinity River Improvement Association. He was active in the Rivercrest Country Club, the Fort Worth Club, and the Dallas Athletic Club, and during World War II, Fender served as the company's chief executive officer, a dollar-a-year man heading the federal government's fuel administration, and president of the Structural Clay Products Institute. When James E. Fender retired in 1959 at the age of seventy-six, it was clear to fellow Acme associates that an era was ending at Acme Brick Company.

headquarters contained 22,800 square feet of office space. It was air-conditioned, had a one-hundred-seat assembly room, boasted a snack bar for its eighty-five employees, and was built entirely of brick and tile. All the building brick for the new headquarters was provided by the Denton Plant. The brick were pink and buff colors of all the various shapes made by the company.

A worker (lower right) uses automatic lift equipment at the Fort Worth Sales Office in the late 1950s.

A worker on a Clark Propane Forklift in the foreground stacks residential King Size Brick, circa 1950s.

The Pug Mill ran a story introducing the new King Size Brick, circa early 1950s.

9⅝" × 2⅝"

Acme KING SIZE brick is here and it's the answer to a builder's prayer!

An early 1950s advertisement for Acme's revolutionary King Size Brick.

As the 1950s continued, Acme Brick looked for new ways to grow its operation and its reach into new locations and markets. In 1954, Acme Brick furthered its expansion into the Kansas-Missouri market with the purchase of Buffalo Brick and Tile in Buffalo, Kansas. The plant's tremendous asset was its great clay reserves, which were estimated to be sufficient for five hundred years of production.

Acme Brick proceeded to purchase plants in Alexandria, Louisiana, and Waskom, Texas, from Tri-State Brick Company in 1954 as well. While Waskom was the better of the two plants (with a workforce of more than sixty that produced four times the 4 million bricks that Alexandria produced with twenty-one employees), both plants were located in important trade areas. Both plants had to be remodeled, operating for less than ten years before being closed down by mid-1962. As a result of these acquisitions and other strategic moves, net worth in 1955 had nearly doubled from what it had been in 1949. Cash surplus grew from around $700,000 to $3,588,000, a remarkable feat.

In 1958, Acme Brick Company continued its further expansion into Kansas when it acquired brick plants at

The 1956 Bennett Plant addition; the downdraft kilns pictured improved production by 20 percent.

The Bennett Plant
circa 1940.

Forklifts, like this one in use at the Denver Plant in the 1950s, were one of the manufacturing technologies that had been perfected during World War II.

Kanopolis and Great Bend from Great Bend Brick and Tile, a company founded in 1947. The Kanopolis Plant was located near a historic route and community. Built in 1954, the Kanopolis Plant in Ellsworth County was new and modern. Workers would stack brick directly onto kiln cars before drying and burning them in an Allied Tunnel Kiln that was 305 feet long. Forklift trucks did all the intraplant transportation in

Kanopolis, as well as the loading and unloading of kiln cars, trucks, and railroad cars. "The thoroughly modern procedures at this plant helped to set standards for other Acme operations, although the Kanopolis facility was only a year old when Acme obtained it," notes a historical account of the plant.[8]

By the end of the 1950s, Acme Brick was clearly in a period of great growth and economic stability. The company had

Workers perform kiln maintenance, circa the late 1950s.

The company's Safety Logo in the 1950s.

nineteen manufacturing plants and thirty-two sales offices in its five-state area and was producing and selling 300 million brick per year, with a net worth of nearly $10 million. The company had an expanded Board of Directors with a new organization and defined responsibilities. But the end of the 1950s also marked the end of a legendary leader's career at Acme Brick Company. James Ernest Fender, president of Acme Brick Company, retired in 1959 at the age of seventy-six. He had served the company for nearly fifty-three years, and after his retirement, it was noted in a history of the company that "an era had ended."[9] Acme Brick's leadership and employees would have to begin a new decade with a new president and new top-level personnel.

CHAPTER 4
GROWTH YEARS
1960 TO 1969

Like the previous postwar decade, the 1960s were a time of growth and prosperity for Acme Brick Company. The company restructured its management organization, filling the role of president with two different men in the decade. As a result of the emergence of an energy-based economy and subsequent housing boom in Texas and the Southwest during these years, the company experienced great growth and expansion. It acquired new companies and renovated old plants, even diversifying its operations by acquiring nonbrick entities for the first time in its history.

A New Decade, New Presidents

In 1959, Acme experienced great turnover in top-level personnel and management, unprecedented in the company's history up to that point. Looking for Ernest Fender's successor, the Board in 1959 elected Neil Boldrick president. Born in Denison, Texas, on September 7, 1901, Boldrick graduated from high school in 1918 prior to attending the University of Texas. While a student, Boldrick also worked at a Denison bank. He married Laura West in 1923, having graduated college while he was working at a Dallas cotton firm. He went to work at Acme Brick as a salesman in 1925, becoming a regional sales manager in the early 1930s. Boldrick was soon placed in charge of the Houston area and then replaced George Puls as general sales manager, soon becoming vice president.

Besides naming Boldrick president, the Board began the 1960s with several other top-level management decisions. The position of advisory director for each retired president was formed. Also, an Executive Committee was formed that consisted of the chairman and two other Board members. After only a few months, all vice presidential positions were abolished. The new organization that emerged in 1960 was a line organization consisting of several new positions, many of which were recommended (and filled) by a consulting firm.

As his first order of business as president, Neil Boldrick launched a general improvement program that attempted to strengthen the company so that it might have the "vitality to increase its stature as an industry leader in our changing economy."[1] Boldrick spent his time on internal improvements, reducing the company debt to zero and putting almost $750,000 into capital improvements. A number of changes were made under his leadership, which included: the adoption of a new

A worker, left center, checks a stack of brick at the Perla Plant.

salesmen's incentive plan; the approval of more market research; the elimination of the fifth-floor penthouse at the General Office Building; and new advertising and public relations programs. Operationally, Boldrick presided over the modernization of the Malvern facilities (for $800,000); the completion of a plant survey; the purchase of new mechanical handling equipment for drayage operation; the introduction of a new machine accounting system; the opening of a new sales office in El Paso; the completion of a temporary laboratory at Denton; and the establishment of a Ceramic Cooling Tower Division.

Unfortunately for Boldrick, sales significantly dropped in 1960 and 1961, with net profits falling to their lowest level since 1947. The profit shortfall was partly due to a one-time occurrence, a tax bill of $337,000 owed the federal government. Manufacturing costs rose while sales turned downward due to a general decline in construction, and the company lost a number of valuable people who knew the brick business well. By 1961, the company seemed to be in its first downward spiral since the Great Depression.

The February 1961 Stockholders' Meeting would be an important event in the company's history, as it witnessed the election of another president. At the meeting, Acme had the largest number of stockholders in its history (from two men in 1890 to 186 by 1930, to 300 by 1950, and to 596 by 1961). Chairman Neil Boldrick blocked an attempt by former officers and directors to oust one particular Board member. In response to that decision, the Board moved forward on its improvement programs by installing a new president and a new Finance Department that summer. The Board selected the relatively young D. O. Tomlin, an energetic executive, to take on the duties of managing the company as president.

A native Texan who graduated from Southern Methodist University in 1936 with a degree in finance and banking, D. O. Tomlin was an extremely bright and driven young man. After graduating college, he completed two years of graduate work at the Harvard Business School, majoring in sales management. His first job was with the American Zinc, Lead, and Smelting Company in 1937. He later became treasurer of Briggs-Weaver Machinery Company of Dallas in 1946. Over the years, Tomlin had been president of the Dearborn Stove Company, the Lone Star Boat Company, and several professional associations (such as the Outboard Boat Manufacturers Association, the Dallas Manufacturers and Wholesale Association, the Texas Manufacturers Association, and the Dallas Personnel Association). Tomlin had a wide variety of interests outside of work, serving as the director in several banks and a half-dozen

civic associations while also acting as an advisor to the Board of the University of Dallas, the Boy Scouts of America, the Highland Park Methodist Church, and a local school for the deaf. Like many other Acme presidents, he also was a member of the River Crest Country Club and the Fort Worth Club.

When D. O. Tomlin went to work at Acme Brick on August 15, 1961, he had never seen the inside of a brick plant. But it could not be ignored that at the age of forty-six, Tomlin brought "an outstanding combination of academic preparation and experience to Acme."[2] For eight years, Tomlin acted as president of Acme, a time that was marked by great change. Shortly after taking over as president, Tomlin set up a new structure, both in management and in sales, for increased profits and improved customer service. He consolidated manufacturing activities in Kansas at Kanopolis, reshuffled the physical arrangement of the home office, encouraged the release of the first company magazine in thirty years, and visited every plant and sales office. To visit every plant and sales office in 1961 was an intense and busy endeavor, as Acme had nineteen plants, thirty-two sales offices, and was selling 300 million brick annually during this time.

Still, in 1961, Acme's profits were the lowest they had been since the Great Depression. Tomlin reacted by introducing several austerity measures during the first eighteen months of his presidency. He discontinued operations at the Alexandria Plant and consolidated other operations (especially those in Kansas). He closed down the Great Bend Plant in November 1961 and the Waskom Plant three months later, both of which were old facilities with poor safety records that duplicated products made in other company units. Tomlin closed sales offices at El Paso, Texas; Hot Springs, Arkansas; and Houma, Louisiana. His revised Credit Department operations brought gains in collections. Tomlin's changes also included a renewed focus on safety promotion, and new marketing efforts, including a new single-order entry system that improved the flow between sales and production. All these measures yielded good results for the company, as sales volumes quickly picked up in 1962. With D. O. Tomlin at the wheel, Acme Brick was poised for productive years to come.

Acme Brick Expands and Diversifies

As Acme Brick experienced top-level personnel changes and implemented improvement plans in the early 1960s, the state of Texas and the Southwest region were booming. Fueled by an energy-based economy, an expanded Interstate Highway System, and a residential housing boom, the region had been experiencing a profound period of industrial growth since World War II. This industrialization brought with it the growth of the construction business, the rise of defense industries, and the expansion of petrochemical facilities in the region. The oil and gas industry had been critical to the economic growth of Texas and other Southwestern states during this time,[3] as was the National Interstate and Defense Highway Act of 1956. That influential legislation, signed into law by President Dwight D. Eisenhower on June 29, 1956, set up a forty-thousand-mile Interstate Highway System that connected two coasts. President Eisenhower, a proponent of a large-scale interregional highway system, witnessed firsthand as a general during World War II the advantages that Germany enjoyed because of the impressive autobahn network. Industrial and transportation growth was accompanied by a booming residential housing industry. For these reasons, Acme Brick geared up for a particularly productive decade in the early 1960s.

In 1960 and 1961, Tomlin and Acme Brick Company replaced inefficient production with more modern facilities. Acme Brick began a period of several years of expansion, acquiring companies that enhanced its brick output and those that diversified the company's product base. In late 1960, Acme Brick began negotiations for the purchase of Fraser Brick and Tile Company of San Antonio, Texas. It completed the acquisition in early 1961, at a cost of $750,000. This gave Acme Brick a total of twenty operating brickworks.

Another display of Acme's expansion in the early 1960s was the acquisition of the United Brick Division of Martin-Marietta in February 1963, which brought with it a number of plants in Missouri, Kansas, and Oklahoma. The seven plants were located in Kansas City, Missouri; Harrisonville, Missouri; Weir, Kansas; Tulsa, Oklahoma; Oklahoma City, Oklahoma; Collinsville, Oklahoma; and Coffeyville, Kansas. Acme Brick also welcomed 230 new employees and an entry into the market areas of the United plants, leading the company to open a new sales office at Springfield, Missouri.

United Brick and Tile Company of Independence, Kansas, had a rich history. It was an old company as well as an Acme Brick rival at one time. United had merged with Coffeyville Vitrified Brick and Tile in the 1920s, whose brick plant in Coffeyville had been an important part of the brick industry. In fact, Coffeyville Vitrified Brick and Tile had marketed its bricks around the world. Prior to Acme Brick's acquisition, United had been bought out by the Martin-Marietta Corporation. The Chicago firm's management expected a profit of nearly 12 percent, but when a slight construction slump hit in 1960, the conglomerate began seeking buyers for the division. Acme Brick, which sought a stronger sales position in the Kansas-Missouri market area, jumped at the first opportune moment when Martin-Marietta put those plants up for purchase.

A burner at an Acme Brick Plant checks kiln temperature control, circa the 1960s.

A worker unloads a round kiln, circa the 1960s.

White Brick emerging from a kiln at Perla.

Acme Brick Company further showed its impressive growth in the mid-1960s when it renovated and opened the state-of-the-art Denton Plant. Acme Brick laid plans and started the construction of the new building in 1962, opening the new plant in October 1963. The opening was a major event in Denton, with the company providing guided tours, refreshments, and amateur and professional bricklaying contest for guests. The grand opening even featured a fireworks display on Halloween night. As a history of Acme noted, the company had "pulled out all the stops" in promoting the new Denton Plant, as well as "to get the public interested in the brick industry and make them aware of its importance to the community."[4]

The new plant at Denton, built to be "the ideal brick plant," was one of the most modern plants in the nation.[5] With more than 160,000 square feet of manufacturing floor space, the plant

Unloading brick from the Perla Plant in the 1960s.

had an annual capacity of over 25 million brick (and later, with new kilns, 60 million brick a year). Acme equipped the site with all the latest machinery, specially designing a Harrop Kiln more than 380 feet long. The plant initially encountered problems in shrinkage control in the earliest months of its operation, but those problems were solved. The Denton Tunnel Kiln "B" was added in July 1965 and Tunnel Kiln "C" in March 1967, leading to the old Denton Plant (which had operated since 1917) to close down for good in 1967. Around this same time, Acme also opened the fully automated East Gate Plant at Perla, Arkansas ("Perla No. 3") in late 1967, having closed its refractory business at Perla in the early 1960s.

A Six-State System

By the middle of the decade, Acme Brick Company seemed to be on a roll. The company had become a six-state system that extended over four regional areas, operating twenty-three brick and tile manufacturing installations in Arkansas, Kansas, Louisiana, Oklahoma, Missouri, and Texas. It had twenty-nine branch offices, and in 1965 shipments reached a peak of 433 million brick. The company had an ownership of 300,000 shares distributed among 504 stockholders in nineteen states,

the Bahamas, and the District of Columbia. For five years from 1963 to 1968, Acme enjoyed one of the most prosperous periods in its history.

By the late 1960s, Acme Brick had also redefined its product line and expanded its role in the construction business. It increased sales of several lines of brick during this time, including "the King Size" Brick, "Classic," "Old Time," and many other brick shapes. The King Size Brick remains the

Workers at the Fort Smith Plant show off their Service Award in December 1965; note the near universal use of hard hats.

Acme Brick hosts an architect's meeting at Fort Worth in 1962.

dominant size for residential construction in the twenty-first century and was a tremendous innovation sixty years ago. The company emphasized home construction during the 1960s, helping develop the idea of double-wall construction completely of brick for building multistory apartments and for buildings without use of steel and concrete frames. It dropped the production of fire brick and concentrated on developing its face brick lines, leading it to become the largest producer of face brick in the nation by 1965 (making and selling over two-and-a-half times the number of brick it had made in 1928). Still, major changes were still ahead for the company as the decade came to a close.

Diversifying the Product Base

In the late 1960s, President D. O. Tomlin decided to diversify the company's product base, an unprecedented move for the brick company. Brick had begun to receive increased competition from concrete, asbestos cement, aluminum, steel, plastic, and cheap imported adobe brick, though most still preferred the quality advantages of brick in the home construction market. Regardless of the preferences of some, it was clear to many larger brick manufacturers (like Acme Brick) that diversifying products was necessary. While Acme Brick did increase its brick production, it also acquired new companies with products different than brick to "deal effectively with competing materials such as lightweight aggregate blocks and

The New Tunnel Kiln at Denton, Texas Was Dynamite from the Word 'Go'

D.O. Tomlin and John Justin Signed Merger Agreement Which Placed Acme Brick and Justin Boots Under the Same Ownership.

Acme Expanded its Sales of Endicott Clay Products.

Endicott

Neil Armstrong Took A Giant Step for Mankind

Proud Americans Served in Vietnam.

In 1991, Acme Brick created a centennial advertisement to celebrate the events of the 1960s.

cinder blocks, and precast and prestressed concrete."[6]

Acme Brick Company made its first nonbrick acquisition when it purchased Nolan Browne Company, a Dallas-based concrete block manufacturer on March 1, 1968. The company had begun its operation in 1934, when Nolan Browne, Sr., bought the equipment of a defunct concrete company for $3,400. The only products it made at that time were sand-and-gravel concrete blocks. The company eventually grew into a thriving business, with annual sales above $1 million. The company held patents on "Featherlite" (expanded shale aggregate) and a manufacturing license for "Spectra-Glaze," a specially coated block resembling tile that Acme Brick hoped to sell.

That same year, Acme followed the acquisition of Nolan Browne Company with the purchase of McDonald Brothers Cast Stone Company of Fort Worth. Originally founded in 1920 as the C. J. Sutton Company, the company first manufactured only concrete block. But by the time of its purchase by Acme, the company was the largest manufacturer of engineered precast products in the Southwest, making precast concrete panels and cast stone products. The deal to purchase McDonald Brothers was financed partly by cash, liberal stock options, and guaranteed employment for the three principle owners.

Acme Brick still looked elsewhere to diversify its products base, proceeding to purchase United Cement Products Company and Born Block, both of Wichita, Kansas. With

D. O. Tomlin, left, and John Justin sign the merger agreement in 1969.

THE CORPORATE HISTORY OF THE JUSTIN COMPANIES

Since the nineteenth century, Justin Companies was known nationally and worldwide for its high-quality cowboy boots. The company made a variety of other casual footwear, including the popular Wellington-style boot. Its founder, H. J. Justin, had come to Texas in 1879 from Missouri. That year, he made a pair of boots for a thoroughly impressed cowboy who spread the word of his bootmaking skills. The demand for boots was high, and after setting up shop on the Chisholm Trail, he eventually moved the company to Fort Worth in 1925. At that time, the Justin Company was doing over $200,000 worth of business. For comparison, the company had done $12,000 at best in the 1910s.

The Justin Companies were a family affair. John Sullivan Justin, Sr., went to work for his father in 1901 at the age of twelve, eventually becoming a full partner in the business just seven years later. By 1931, the company was making shoes as well as boots. Besides the boot company that founded in 1879, the Justin family also owned the Justin Leather Goods Company, which was organized in 1917. This company, along with John S. Justin, Jr.'s Justin Belt Company, produced western dress, casual belts, handcrafted wallets, purses, key cases, and other leather items. Justin companies' goods sold through a network of approximately nine thousand authorized dealers.

In 1938, John S. Justin, Jr., had gone into business on his own, forming the Justin Barton Belt Company with a partner. He changed the name to the Justin Belt Company in 1943 when he bought out his partner. Seven years later, he joined his father's company, H. J. Justin and Sons in 1950, a company that had been started by John S. Justin, Jr.'s grandfather years before Acme Brick was founded. Two years later he became its president, at which time he applied principles that made his own enterprise successful. The Justin Companies increased outlets, marketed Justin products in South America, and formed the Fort Worth Boot Company (which distributed children's cowboy boots).

Because of its rich history and strategic corporate maneuvers in the 1950s and 1960s, the Justin Companies were an impressive addition to the First Worth Corporation in its earliest years. Not surprisingly, the Justin Companies were one of the lone bright spots in the first years of the holding company's existence.

these moves, Acme Brick acquired one of the best local Wichita concrete block companies and a statewide franchise on Spectra-Glaze block and other precast products. As Tomlin told stockholders in June 1968, "putting the block and brick business together there enables us to serve our customers much more efficiently and effectively."[7]

A White Freightliner with a tandem trailer in front of Acme Brick's corporate office in Fort Worth, circa the 1960s.

Still unfinished with diversification, Acme purchased two more companies in the late 1960s. Since the McDonald Company owned 50 percent of ACF PreCast Products, Inc., of Lubbock, Texas, Acme decided to buy out the remaining stock of that company as well. That same month, Acme also purchased Concrete Casting Corporation of Arkansas, located in North Little Rock. The company supplied precast concrete panels and prestressed concrete products to a statewide market.

But by the time that Acme Brick emerged from its 1968 round of acquisitions, the company itself merges with the Justin companies and becomes part of First Worth Corporation. It would continue its growth into the 1970s as a key component of Justin's First Worth Corporation.

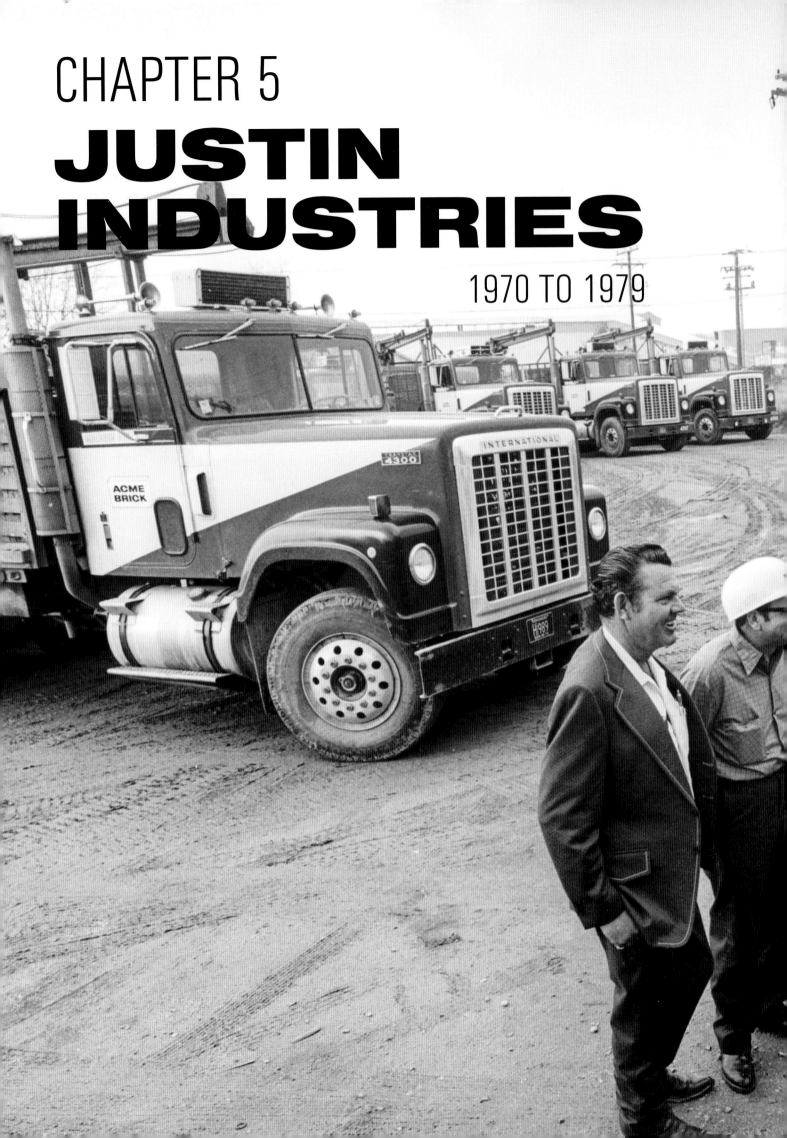

CHAPTER 5
JUSTIN INDUSTRIES
1970 TO 1979

John Koch, Acme Brick's head of production and considered by many in the industry to be the best brickmaker in the United States, shows off a Colonial Brick from the company's brick collection.

Readers of the *Fort Worth Star-Telegram* glanced at a front-page story on the morning of November 22, 1968, commemorating the fifth anniversary of the assassination of President John F. Kennedy in nearby Dallas. On the same page was a three-column photograph of John Justin and D. O. Tomlin shaking hands in front of a background of boots and brick.

Star-Telegram Business Editor Harold Monroe reported that "two of Fort Worth's oldest manufacturing companies—perhaps the two very oldest—joined Thursday under the aegis of a three-month-old corporation that bids fair to become a conglomerate."[1]

The formation of First Worth Corporation was a longtime dream of Tomlin, the Harvard graduate who rode the Texas boom of the 1960s into a brick and stone conglomerate. The

Drivers, supervisors, and sales personnel confer at the Perla Plant, 1973.

After the merger with Justin Boot, the Fort Worth headquarters was renamed First Worth Corporation; the windows are for access of firemen per the Fort Worth Fire Code.

Star-Telegram's Monroe agreed with Tomlin's vision. "Acme Brick," he wrote, "already a wholly-owned division of First Worth Corporation, and Justin Boot will become one."[2]

The merger had been set up so that both entities would remain essentially autonomous. Sproesser Wynn, the Fort Worth attorney who had helped Tomlin create First Worth Corporation, had been instrumental in convincing Justin that the merger agreement made sense. Early in 1968, Wynn had suggested to Justin that he consider merging with First Worth. Justin Boot, and its owner John Justin, had huge potential tax liabilities. "The way things were at that time," Justin explained in the mid-1990s, "my Justin stock had no fixed value because it wasn't being traded. If something happened to me, it would have to be evaluated by the Internal Revenue Service, and I knew it would be pretty high because the company was a good

moneymaker even though all of the money was being put back into it. There would be a lot of taxes due."[3]

"It Sounded Like a Pretty Good Idea"

Justin's major fear at the time was that his wife, Jane, would have to sell the company to pay the taxes should anything happen to him.

So when Wynn put him together with Tomlin, Justin was more than willing to listen. "It sounded like a pretty good idea," he said. "First Worth had plans for a new stock issue that would pave the way for it to apply for a listing on the New York Stock Exchange. They were already preparing the application to the Securities and Exchange Commission for the stock offering. Going on the New York Stock Exchange would at least give my stock a value. I could sell some of it if I wanted to."[4]

Justin was initially impressed with Tomlin's vision. "Tomlin wanted to make a deal," he said. "He painted a pretty good picture for me of what they were planning to do."[5] Acme Brick Company had recently purchased Louisiana Concrete Products Company, as well as a concrete company located in Wichita, Kansas. "They had some ambitious plans for expansion and diversification," he said. "It all sounded pretty good, so I agreed to a deal."[6]

The deal called for First Worth Corporation to acquire all of the outstanding capital stock of H. J. Justin and Sons. In exchange, First Worth would issue Justin 72,225 shares of its stock. Another 37,775 shares of First Worth stock would be issued to Justin in exchange for the Justin Leather Goods Company, a subsidiary of H. J. Justin and Sons. Tomlin guaranteed Justin that if the price of First Worth Corporation stock fell to $23 or less three years after the 1968 merger, Justin would be entitled to additional stock of First Worth to make up for the loss in value.

Struggling with Profits and Expenses

When Justin agreed to the merger with First Worth Corporation in late 1968, Acme was coming off a very strong year. Acme Brick's shipments for 1968 were at a new high of 440 million brick equivalent (MBE), but that would be the last good news the company would report for more than a year. As a holding company, First Worth was liable to federal tax surcharges; those surcharges were equal in 1968 to the entire federal tax Acme Brick had paid the year before.[7]

The administration of President Richard M. Nixon and the beginnings of disengagement from the War in Vietnam upset the guns and butter economy that President Lyndon Johnson had tried to finesse through the mid-1960s. The result was a dramatic drop in construction, which was quickly reflected in brick sales and shipments. In 1969, the company reported 400 MBE, a 10 percent drop from the year previous.[8] As a result of the slump, First Worth closed Acme Brick plants in Oklahoma City, Oklahoma; Harrisonville, Missouri; and Ferris, Texas, during 1969. Meanwhile, the expenses associated with the recent acquisitions that formed the concrete division were eating into profits.

Coupled with the drop in housing starts, which impacted the sale of brick, Acme was trying to integrate a number of acquisitions it had made in the past year. Most were not brick operations, but were concrete architectural panel, prestressed concrete, and concrete block companies. Acme Brick Company had made a substantial cash outlay for the acquisitions, and was finding it difficult to match them up with proper management talent.

While Acme Brick Company was struggling with profits and expenses, First Worth Corporation made an ill-timed decision to go ahead with a public offering early in 1969. The effort was abandoned in July 1969, but not before First Worth had racked up another $139,000 in consulting fees and other expenses. Meanwhile, John Justin was growing more concerned by the day.

He felt that there had been misrepresentation about the assets and performance of First Worth Corporation, and that the Justin Companies were keeping the holding company afloat in 1969. Justin was further concerned that he was being represented by Sproesser Wynn, the Fort Worth attorney who also represented First Worth. In 1969, Justin went to the Fort Worth National Bank Building to see an up-and-coming attorney named Dee Kelly.[9]

"Dee's office was so small there was barely room for his desk and chair and the two chairs (Howard) Jennings and I occupied," Justin told an interviewer years later. But the two men, hit it off, and Kelly agreed to represent Justin. Kelly's advice was simple: Justin should sue to overturn the merger agreement.[10]

Before Justin's suit could gain much traction, however, J. Olcott Phillips, Sproesser's partner in the Fort Worth firm of McDonald, Sanders, Wynn, Ginsburg, Phillips and Maddox, approached Kelly. Phillips had replaced Sproesser as First Worth's attorney, and he brought an offer to make Justin president and CEO of First Worth Corporation. Kelly advised Justin to reject the offer, continue with the suit, and get his company back.

"I Gave It a Lot of Thought"

"I thought that was the more conservative approach," Kelly said years later. "But John had better judgment than I did. He declined my advice, and he accepted the offer."[11]

Justin's reasoning was simple. If he sued and won, First Worth would likely appeal, tying the merger up in litigation for years. "I gave it a lot of thought," he said, "and I finally decided my best course was to take over management of the company and try to pull it out."[12]

A local business writer observed at the time that calling 1969 a reversal or setback for First Worth was understating the magnitude of the company's problems. "In reality," he said, "the slump more closely resembled a wounded bomber, its wings shot off, spiraling flames in its earthward plunge." The reality, however, was somewhat different from what the local media perceived. First Worth was a cyclical business, and its Acme Brick operations did not even lose money that year.

Worker on the line at the Denton Plant, circa the 1970s.

As the largest stockholder in the company, Justin backed the election of a new slate of directors. At a contentious Board meeting in November 1969, the Board replaced Tomlin with Justin. It was that meeting that Ed Stout recalled years later as "the bloodletting."[13] Before the dust had settled in early 1970, Tomlin, three vice presidents and most of the old Board of Directors were gone. Stout was one of two Acme Brick vice presidents remaining. He would be there in the next several years to help Justin pull First Worth out of its slump.

"A Real Big Challenge"

Justin's first choice to replace Tomlin as president of Acme Brick Company resigned after several months to operate his own brick business. "I didn't have anyone to run the brick business," Justin said. "So I took over as president of Acme Brick."[14] He soon discovered that the brick business and the boot business had some similarities.

"I knew I was facing a challenge, a real big challenge," he said. "I felt that I knew how to run a company and how to work with people but the brick business was entirely new to me."[15]

But Justin realized that marketing brick wasn't really all that different from selling boots. "Both are sold by displaying them to customers," he said. "People buy brick and boots with their eyes."[16] He explained that he was fascinated when women visited an Acme

Brick sales office two or three days in a row trying to narrow down the brick she wanted for the new home she was building. "She'll look at one brick and then she'll look at the other and then she'll say 'I like this one a little better. That one's a little too brown. I sure like the texture on this one.'"[17]

Justin could relate, because that was how people bought boots. And he came to the realization that boots and brick weren't really all that different in the way they were made. Boots were made from leather, and no two pieces of leather were ever exactly alike. As a result, they had to be cut differently. Brick, Justin determined, was similar, in that brick was made out of clay, and no two clay deposits were exactly the same.[18]

Management by Walking Around

Justin taught himself the brick business in the early 1970s by donning an old pair of jeans and a scuffed pair of boots and driving out to an Acme Brick plant in the Fort Worth area. "You'd be surprised by how much information you can get that way," he said. "I learned how they mixed the clay and how they extruded it, all those kinds of things. It was a constant learning process."[19]

Justin's version of management by walking around hadn't been seen much at the company's brick plants since the end of World War II. And the new president of the company soon discovered that Acme Brick salesmen were hesitant to sell brick from the company's Denton Plant because of inconsistency in color. On large orders, they said, brick would change color, causing problems with customers. Denton served the flagship Dallas–Fort Worth market, and Justin was determined to get to the bottom of what had become a major problem by 1971.

The new president made several trips to the Denton Plant seeking answers. One operator suggested that the company's basic strategy of mining clay was at fault. He told Justin the clays were undulating in the ground and needed to be mined in what he called a layer-cake process. Justin authorized the purchase of a front-end loader and scraper to aid in the mining. The problem of inconsistency quickly disappeared, and brick from the Denton Plant became a staple in the Dallas–Fort Worth market for the next forty-plus years.

Justin told colleagues that one thing he understood very well was the process of manufacturing, following a lifetime in the boot business. He quickly gained a comfort level with brickmaking. Justin also was a keen judge of talent. And he grew to rely on the advice and counsel of Ed Stout, who had been one of the few Acme Brick Company executives to survive the bloodletting of late 1969.

Workers dehacking brick in the 1970s at the Denton Plant; the monorail is in the background.

A gas-fired Harrop Kiln at the Denton Plant in the 1970s.

A worker at the Denton Plant in 1977, easily handling fifty pounds of brick.

Duane Bequette, burner operator at the Denton Plant, in 1977.

Brickmaking at the Denton Plant was as labor intensive in 1975 as it was three-quarters of a century before.

A 1975 Denton Plant packaging machine that is still in use in 2016.

By late 1970, Stout was advising Justin that the cyclical nature of the brick business was pointing to the need for the company to build inventory to meet demand for a recovery in the early 1970s. At a series of meetings in the fourth quarter of 1970, Stout pointed out that the brick business "had always been very cyclical and that, historically, except for the Great Depression, the down cycles usually lasted from eighteen to thirty months. Then there would be a year of buildup and a year or two of high activity before the next down cycle began. We have records dating back to 1917 that show that to be pretty consistent. Some of us felt that the market had to turn around. It had been down for over a year and a half, pushing two years."[20]

Justin made the decision to begin building inventory, and this was very much the right decision. Building began to pick up in early 1971, and didn't stop growing for the next two years. "We went into 1971 with our wagon loaded and were able to capitalize on a good year," Justin recalled years later.[21] Interest rates dropped steadily throughout the period, encouraging new construction. Both the brick and the concrete divisions reported banner years in 1971, and bettered their performance in 1972. Acme Brick continued modernization efforts and reopened the Oklahoma City Plant in 1972 to meet the increased demand for brick. First Worth stock was a direct beneficiary of the recovery, nearly doubling in value from 1971 to 1972.[22]

First Worth Corporation's turnaround year was 1972. Justin reported to shareholders in early 1973 that the boots and brick conglomerate's 1972 sales had topped $63 million, and that net income had increased by 65 percent from 1971. He also noted that the company had changed its name to Justin Industries, Inc., and he had assumed the position of Chairman of the Board of the newly renamed holding company. Replacing Justin as President of the Acme Brick Company subsidiary was industry veteran Edward L. Stout.[23]

"Mr. Brick"

In the three years since assuming control of Justin Industries, John Justin had come to rely heavily on Ed Stout's business savvy. In introducing Stout as the new president of Acme Brick Company, Justin referred to his choice as "Mr. Brick." Stout, he said, "knows more about the brick business than anybody I know."[24]

Stout had been working side-by-side with Justin ever since early 1971. Justin knew Stout could sell brick—something he had been doing for nearly a quarter-century—but he needed him in Fort Worth to handle brick production. Stout protested that he knew relatively little about production.

An Acme Brick salesman (right) visits the Perla Plant in 1973.

"Well that's good," Justin said. "You can learn."[25]

Stout spearheaded the company's quick recovery in 1971 and 1972. Justin was so impressed that he tapped Stout as president of Acme Brick Company in February 1973.

As it was, Justin was doing Stout no favors. Barely eight months into his tenure as president, Stout faced his first crisis. The Yom Kippur War between Israel and its Arab neighbors that October unleashed a trade war. The Organization of Petroleum Exporting Countries (OPEC), mainly Middle Eastern oil producers, embargoed the shipment of oil to the United States because of the country's support of Israel during the recent hostilities. Cut off from

its major supplier of foreign oil, the United States struggled to contain inflation. The price of oil and gas quadrupled in a short period of time. Meanwhile, the Nixon Administration was consumed with the Watergate crisis.

From Recession to Recovery

When President Richard M. Nixon resigned in August 1974 to be replaced by Vice President Gerald Ford, the nation was in the throes of another recession. Housing starts dropped below 170,000 in 1975, a lower level than during the recession of 1969 and 1970, and inflation and unemployment were both recorded in double digits. Brick shipments slipped to their lowest point

Above: Acme Brick used White Trucks with tandem trailers through most of the 1970s.

Right: In the late 1970s, Acme Brick began purchasing International Trucks and tandem trailers for its fleet.

Dehacking brick in the 1970s; the implementation of Occupational Safety and Health Administration (OSHA) regulations during the decade required workers to don hard hats and safety glasses when on the line.

This 1991 centennial advertisement paid tribute to the 1970s.

Labels within the illustration:
Computer Controls Brickmaking
The Nixon Administration
Gas Rationing Created Long Lines at Service Stations.
Acme Launches Advertising Program
Acme Expanded its Product Line to Include a Wide Variety of Masonry Products.
The Bicentennial Celebration Featured Operation Sail.
ACME BRICK. THE BEST THING TO HAVE AROUND YOUR HOUSE.

since 1970 in 1975, but Acme Brick weathered the recession surprisingly well. The company had been focused on productivity since 1971, and it had strengthened its sales organization and production capability dramatically during the first half of the decade. Profits were far above those of the difficult years at the beginning of the decade, and Acme Brick was well poised to take advantage of the coming economic recovery.[24]

That recovery began in earnest in 1975 when the Gross National Product (GNP) reported a near 6 percent gain. The GNP registered a 5 percent annual gain through 1978. The gain was reflected in a housing market that rapidly heated up midway through President Jimmy Carter's only term; there were 340,000 housing starts in 1978.[27]

Stout had taken advantage of the energy crisis to address Acme Brick Company's fuel cost issues. Natural gas was the largest cost component in brick manufacturing after labor, and even though Texas and Oklahoma were awash in gas reserves, much of it was regulated and unprofitable to drill and pump in the wake of the 1973 oil embargo. Acme Brick Company began investing in natural gas exploration, which paid off handsomely in the late 1970s and

1980s when Congress began deregulating natural gas exploration and drilling.[28] The company also worked ceaselessly to make the most efficient use of the gas it was burning; during a nine-year period ending in 1978, gas consumption per brick produced dropped a whopping 40 percent.[29]

The increase in productivity during the 1970s made Acme Brick Company a much more nimble and flexible organization. The company was quick to adjust production to demand levels. In 1973, it rebuilt its Tulsa Plant, only to close the facility at the end of 1974 when demand dropped off sharply. It closed its McQueeny, Texas, Plant in August 1975 when the housing market bottomed, and reopened the facility in 1978 when demand increased. Acme Brick Company bought Malvern Brick and Tile in October 1978 to serve the fast-growing Arkansas market, and at the end of that year, the company reopened the Oklahoma City and Ouachita East Plants.[30]

The Fight Against Mexican Brick

In the mid-1970s, Stout and the Acme Brick Company executive management team encountered another threat, this time from outside the company's traditional Southwest market. By 1975, Texas was being inundated with hundreds of millions of substandard Mexican brick. The problem affected homebuilders as well as Acme Brick. Most of the substandard imported brick did not meet building codes, and it began crumbling within months of being laid.

"My first house had Mexican brick, and that was a mistake I never made again," one Dallas resident said years later. "From then on out, I always made sure my house was built of Acme Brick."[31]

Acme Brick Company fought back with a coordinated marketing and branding campaign. Prior to 1975, the company's advertising was primarily industry advertising through the Brick Industry of Texas, a trade association representing the Lone Star State's brick manufacturers. Ed Stout, who supported the Brick Industry of Texas program, felt Acme Brick needed to do more to fight the flood of Mexican brick.

Acme Brick Company developed and ran print and broadcast advertising that acquainted the public with the problems associated with imported brick. Stout asked Harrold E. Melton, a former Acme Brick employee who had just completed his doctorate in finance and was teaching at West Texas State University in Canyon, to return to Acme Brick at Fort Worth and spearhead the company's marketing efforts.[32]

Under Melton's direction, Acme Brick launched the advertising campaign; Mexican brick accounted for as much as 70 percent of market consumption in the Metroplex and Houston.

THE LIFE AND CAREER OF JOHN S. JUSTIN, JR.

John Sullivan Justin, Jr., the founder of Justin Industries, was one of the best-known businessmen in Dallas–Fort Worth. As president of First Worth Corporation, and later Justin Industries, Justin was head of the holding company that owned and operated Acme Brick Company for more than thirty years.

John Justin was heir to one of the oldest businesses in Texas. Justin's grandfather, H. J. "Joe" Justin, began making boots at Spanish Forks on the Red River for cowboys along the Chisholm Trail in 1879. Joe Justin eventually moved to Nocona and founded H. J. Justin and Sons. The sons, John, Earl, and Avis, took over the company in 1916 when Joe Justin became ill, and they moved the company to bigger quarters in Fort Worth in 1925.[1]

Born in Nocona in 1917, Justin grew up in the bootmaking business. He recalled working at the boot company as a schoolboy in Fort Worth during the 1920s, selling ice-cold soft drinks to the workers in the factory.[2] Justin graduated from Central High School and attended Oklahoma A&M College and TCU. In 1938, he started the Justin Belt Company, his first business venture.

During World War II, he served in the U.S. Merchant Marine, and when he returned to Fort Worth from service, he joined the H. J. Justin and Sons Company fulltime. He was named vice president in 1950 and moved up to the presidency in 1953 when his father was named chairman of the Board. By the mid-1950s, the boot company was shipping one hundred thousand pairs of boots from its Fort Worth factory each week, and John Justin, Jr., had opened markets for the company in South America.[3]

Justin changed the name of the company to Justin Boot Company following his father's death in 1959. He had purchased outright ownership of the company from other family members by 1967, and over the years he expanded Justin Boot by acquiring Nocona Boot Company and Tony Lama Boot Company.[4] In 1968, he agreed to merge with Acme Brick Company under the umbrella of First Worth Corporation.[5] The next year, he ousted most of Acme Brick Company's management from First Worth Corporation and renamed the firm Justin Industries Inc.[6]

Far more than a business executive, Justin served as mayor of Fort Worth in 1961 and 1962, and was a pillar of the Metroplex philanthropic community. Justin was a strong backer of the Fort Worth YMCA, United Way–Community Chest, Better Business Bureau, the Opera Association, and the Fort Worth Club. He was an active member of the local Rotary Club, the Double G Club, the Colonial and River Crest Country Clubs, and the Steeplechase Club.[7]

John and Jane Justin, who he married in 1953, were named "Man and Woman of the Year" by the National Cowboy Hall of Fame in Oklahoma City in 1984. Justin was inducted into the Texas Business Hall of Fame and Texas Hall of Honor. In 1992, he received the Charles Goodnight Award for his contributions to the TCU Ranch Management Program. He was inducted into the Pro Rodeo Hall of Fame in 1998.[8]

John S. Justin, Jr., died in Fort Worth on Monday, February 26, 2001. In an obituary in the weekly newspaper in the small Oklahoma town where his grandmother had lived, Justin was described as a man who "always had a smile on his face, boots on his feet, and an open door policy at his home and office, where all were welcome."[9]

Melton encountered pushback from some of the builders, who pointed out that Mexican brick reduced the cost of a $100,000 house by about $500. Some homebuilders threatened to boycott Acme Brick if it went ahead with its advertising campaign.

Melton stood his ground. He told homebuilders that if they boycotted Acme Brick, the company would double the advertising budget. In the process, homebuilders were going to be liable down the road for building houses with a defective product. David Weekley, a prominent homebuilder in the Houston area, agreed with Melton and signed on with the advertising campaign. "I told him it wasn't our advertising program that cost you money," Melton said. "It was your use of defective material."[33]

By the early 1980s, the consumption of Mexican brick in Dallas/Fort Worth and Houston had dropped to about a 10 percent market share. "That was the most successful advertising program I've ever seen," Melton said. "It changed the brick industry in Texas."[34]

Acme Brick Company ended the 1970s on a strong note. Shipments of nearly 550 million brick in 1978 were an all-time record, and the company made a major contribution to Justin Industries' bottom line. In 1979, the holding company reported net sales of $184.5 million, quadruple the $46.5 million Justin Industries had reported in net sales in 1971, its first year in business.[35]

After the strong performance in the 1970s, Acme Brick Company looked forward into the future with confidence. But the 1980s would prove to be a roller coaster ride for the economy in general, and the brick industry in particular.

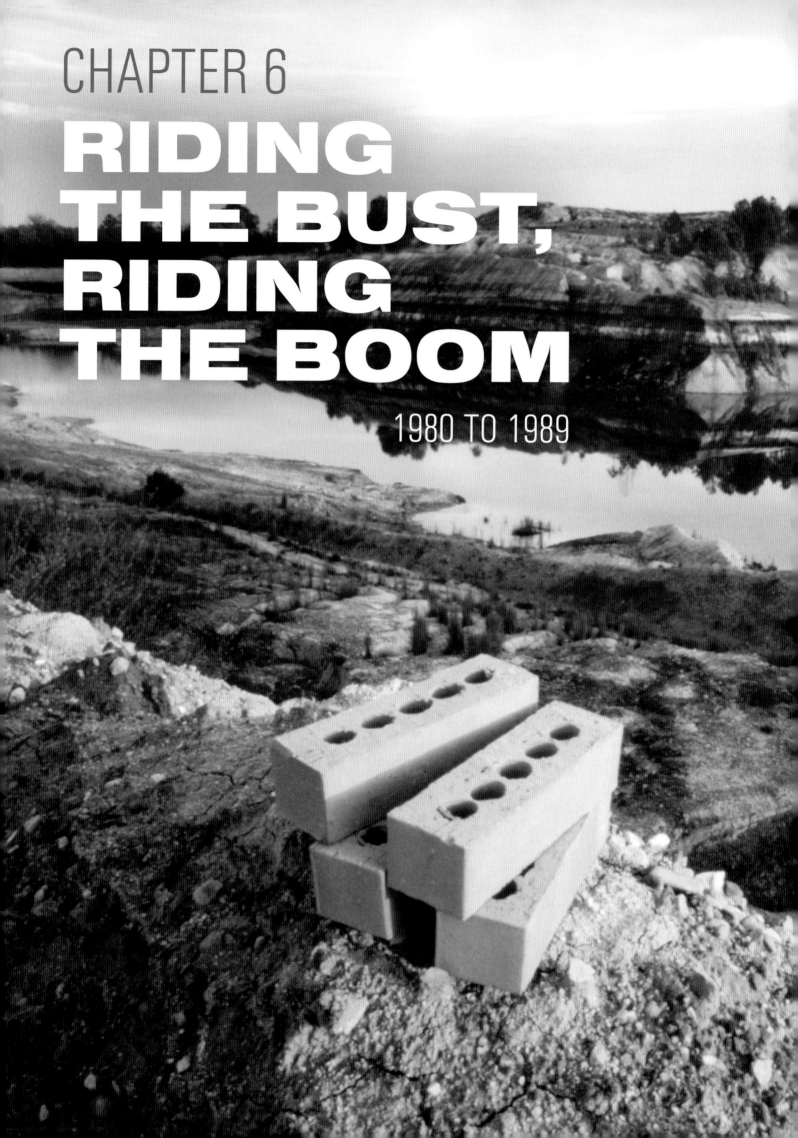

CHAPTER 6
RIDING THE BUST, RIDING THE BOOM
1980 TO 1989

A brick from the first car at the Ouachita Plant, November 1980.

In October 1980, Acme Brick Company held a grand opening ceremony at its newly refurbished Ouachita Plant in Malvern, Arkansas. The community of Malvern, located forty-five miles southwest of Little Rock, advertised itself as "the Brick Capital of the World." Malvern boasted that more brick were produced in the community's three brick plants than in any other known city in the world.[1]

Both Malvern and Acme Brick Company would endure difficult times in the 1980s. The company's Ouachita and Perla Plants in Malvern would be idled and reopened as Acme Brick Company struggled to adjust inventory to fluctuating demand during the decade. The 1980s would open with a severe national recession, pushing housing starts in Texas to a thirty-five-year low in 1981. Acme Brick Company returned to record sales in 1983 and 1984 as Texas and the Southwest emerged from the recession. Sales however fell to another low during the 1988 recession before recovering strongly during the last two years of the decade.

For Malvern and Acme Brick Company, the upheavals that had afflicted the region's brick industry in 1970 and 1971 were dim memories. But they would be revisited just a decade later.

White Brick perched on a bluff overlooking the Perla Pit, circa 1980.

The 1981–1982 Recession

Actually, Texas and the Southwest were late to the recession that began to grip the U.S. economy in 1979. The first to feel the effects of the slowdown was the American iron and steel industry. An industry that had been slow to embrace modernization was hit in 1978 and 1979 by a triple whammy of energy shortages, double-digit inflation and long-term interest rates approaching 15 percent. By the spring of 1980, dozens of iron and coalmines and steel mills had shut down from the Mesabi Range in Minnesota to the Monongahela Valley in Pennsylvania. Thousands of steelworkers were laid off or let go permanently. The nation's busiest U-Haul location was in Hibbing, Minnesota, where several thousand ironworkers packed up and left for a brighter future, many of them headed for the Texas and Oklahoma oilfields.

The nation's Big 3 Automakers quickly followed the steel industry into recession, and by early 1980, Lee Iacocca was using federal loan guarantees to keep Chrysler Corporation out of bankruptcy. The Iranian Revolution that had replaced the Shah of Iran with the Ayatollah Khomeini had unleashed a second energy crisis, and the U.S. dollar traded at its lowest level since the end of World War II. When Ronald Reagan was inaugurated as president in January 1981, inflation was 14 percent a year, and prime interest rates were at 20 percent.[2]

The domestic oil business began to unravel in 1980. Americans had learned how to conserve energy in the wake of the 1973 oil embargo, and that trend had only accelerated following the fall of the Shah of Iran. Natural gas markets were in upheaval as Congress attempted to deregulate a marketplace that had been tightly regulated since the late 1930s. The result was a major recession in the oil patch beginning in late 1980.

That, and the problems in the rest of the economy, quickly translated into a precipitous drop in housing starts. New home construction fell as much as 40 percent as mortgage interest rates settled above 10 percent and stayed there. In 1981, housing starts hit a thirty-five-year low. Instead of hunkering down, Acme Brick Company adjusted production to demand and began building inventory for the inevitable recovery. By the end of 1981, Acme Brick had built up an inventory of more than 400 million brick. The company even expanded, buying the Jamestown, Louisiana and El Dorado, Arkansas Plants from Jamestown Brick and Dixie Brick. Acme Brick never operated the El Dorado Plant, instead consolidating it into the renamed Dixie Plant in Jamestown.[3]

Generations

One reason Acme Brick Company was able to seamlessly adjust product was the expertise and loyalty of its core workforce. Some of the company's workers were multigenerational, the brickmaking legacy passed down from father to son. Arthur Martinez, Jr., is typical of the Acme associate of the last half-century.

Martinez grew up in Bridgeport, forty-five minutes north of Fort Worth, in one of the Acme Brick Company-owned houses. His father, Arthur Martinez, Sr., started at the company in 1945 and worked at Bridgeport until the day he retired in 1982. He had eight brothers, most of whom worked at the Bridgeport Plant.

Arthur Martinez, Jr., remembered as a young man delivering tacos to his father for lunch. "It was mainly a Hispanic community," he said. "Everybody who worked there lived there. Everybody paid rent; daddy paid $3.15 a week. Everybody had beautiful gardens. We all shared the gardens, and you didn't have to lock your door."[4]

Arthur Martinez, Sr., often told his son that what he did at work was "just hard physical labor. They stacked brick by hand in the kiln. It was all done by sections. They would hand-stack green brick. It was one long continuous kiln; the wheelers would haul firebrick out of the kiln with wheelbarrows. Daddy was a setter, setting brick inside the kiln. There were no forklifts in those days."[5]

That specter of hard work did not deter Arthur Martinez, Jr. In 1968, he was working the night shift at a produce company in Fort Worth. He applied for a job at Acme Brick, and as the son of an employee (and nephew of several other employees), he was quickly hired at the Bridgeport Plant. He started on the off-bearing belt, stacking brick on kiln cars. He was part of a five-man crew, and the brick machine never stopped.

For a young man still in his teens, the money was good. The plant operated on a piecework system. Young Martinez and his crew would punch in at 7:00 a.m. and typically work until 3:00 or 3:30 p.m. "Whenever we made our quota for the day," he said of his crew, "we could go home. We did twenty-five to thirty cars a day. The cars were real small, not as big as they are today. And we did have forklifts. But we'd come back the next day and do it all over again."[6]

In 1969, Martinez joined the U.S. Army rather than wait to be drafted. Like many Acme Brick plant employees, he considered it a privilege to serve his country. He volunteered for Airborne and trained at Fort Benning, Georgia, with Special Forces and Army Rangers. He served a thirteen-month tour of duty in Vietnam's I Corps with a Pathfinder detachment;

WELCOME TO ACME BRICK COMPANY "TULSA REDS" GRAND OPENING

The grand opening of Acme Brick's Tulsa Plant, 1985. Ed Stout is right behind the scissors at the ribbon-cutting ceremonies.

pathfinders were always the first into a landing zone (LZ) to provide coordinates for incoming helicopter-borne troops.

"Through Good Brick and Bad Brick"

Martinez returned to the Bridgeport Plant in 1971 and joined a packaging crew. Acme Brick was running at full strength to build up brick inventories in the wake of the 1970 recession, and Martinez and his crew were busy. They used pneumatic tools to strap and band the brick, and forklifts were in greater use. Leather gloves would not hold up to handling brick, so the crews found an innovative solution. They made "palms," circles cut to the outside diameter of their hands from used tire inner tubes, with slits for fingertips.[7]

Martinez worked at Bridgeport for ten years after getting out of the service. In 1981, he left to work in the oil fields north of Fort Worth. By 1986, it was becoming apparent that Texas

oil was going to take years to recover. Hubert Capps, the plant manager at the Denton Plant offered Martinez a job he couldn't refuse: monorail supervisor in the Packaging Department.

Martinez has spent the rest of his career with Acme Brick Company, and has never looked back. And he noted "the thing that has been most important to me in the plant is the people I have worked with, who have gone through good times and bad times, through good brick and bad brick."

Recovery

By 1983, the "Reagan Recovery" was in full swing. Record housing starts, fueled by falling mortgage interest rates, propelled Acme Brick Company to record sales years in both 1983 and 1984. In 1983, the company made and shipped nearly 600 million brick, almost 50 percent more than Acme Brick Company had shipped in 1981. Acme Brick ramped up

A new product meeting in 1983.

production across its system in the mid-1980s. In 1983, the company reopened the Ouachita East Plant in June and the Edmund Plant in December. The Baton Rouge Plant opened early in 1984, and the new Tulsa Plant opened in 1985 to produce architectural brick, special shapes, and pavers.

In 1984, Acme Brick Company solicited bids for construction of a brand-new plant near Sealy, Texas, to serve the booming Houston market. Bidders from the United States, Germany, France, Spain, and Italy competed for the project, and the company finally selected Lingl Corporation from Germany to build the Greenfield Plant off I-10 just west of Houston. The San Felipe Plant was fully automated, and utilized a Pleistocene clay deposit that had stymied brick manufacturers in the past. But eighteen months after being awarded the contract, the German engineers helped Acme Brick plant personnel bring the San Felipe Plant into

During the last eighty years, Acme has produced a variety of paperweights for its customers, like this Texas Sesquicentennial paperweight in 1986.

smooth production of residential brick. On July 28, 1986, the company's first shipment of dark red and brown King Size residential brick began flowing out of the plant.[8]

Everything at the San Felipe Plant was automated. Mining the clay and stacking the brick in the yard were the only two functions at the plant that were not computerized. That was a trend that was already being implemented across the company.

Modernizing the Sales Force

As Acme Brick Company had modernized and streamlined throughout the 1970s and into the 1980s, it had begun to investigate the potential for designing and implementing an information processing and communications system that would link Acme Brick Plants with sales offices and support functions.

As early as 1979, Ed Stout had directed the company's research and development team to begin investigating a way to electronically enter orders and identify inventories quickly. Stout wanted to replace the cumbersome paper order entry system that was making the Acme Brick sales force far less efficient than it could have been.

Jane Justin (left), John Justin, and Ed Stout (with hard hat) present Safety Awards in 1980.

At the time, sales personnel were still doing things the way their predecessors had in the 1950s. There were no cell phones, pagers, fax machines, texts, or e-mail.

Dallas native Brent Snyder started as a sales trainee at the Harry Hines Showroom in 1983. He did inside sales for three months, and then got launched into his own territory in Dallas. "When I first started, there were no pagers," he said. "We were supposed to call into the office four times a day—every two hours or so—to pick up your messages."[9] In the mid-1980s, Snyder was among a group of company sales personnel who got their first cellphones. "It was a Panasonic briefcase phone you

Sales training, like this group session in 1987, became more formalized during the 1980s.

carried in the trunk of your car," he said. "The first cellphone carrier was MetroCell. We were paying thirty-nine cents a minute, so you talked fast."[10]

Greg Hinnrichs, who started with the company several years before Snyder, was assigned the Northeast Texas Territory in 1981, a territory he still serves thirty-five years later. "You didn't get calls all day," he said. "I always had a pocket full of quarters. I can tell you to this day where every pay phone was located in my territory and where the cell coverage cuts out in ten different places across Northeast Texas all the way to Paris."[11]

Mark Burden, a native of Muleshoe, Texas, recalled how essentially unwieldy the company's order entry system was. Burden, who went through sales training in 1985, can remember writing up a brick order on a piece of sheetrock paper. "The customer would hand me the order and I'd type it up on a Smith-Corona electric typewriter. Then you'd hand enter it into a ledger book at night for inventory. You had a three-ring binder with hard manila folder stock for customer cards. There were rotary phones and little pink 'While You Were Out' slips on a spike. It was a very slow pace at the time."[12]

BRIX

In 1983, Acme Brick Company began the multiyear development and implementation of its BRIX system (Brick Reporting and Information exchange), which it identified as "the most comprehensive on-line computerized information system in the industry."[13] BRIX was rolled out over a three-year period and was installed in every company plant and sales office by the end of 1986.

Dennis Knautz, a Chicago-area native who had come to Fort Worth to attend TCU, worked for Bill Lemond at Fort Worth City Transit in the late 1970s. Lemond left for a job

A sales meeting led by Harrold Melton (at head of table) in 1983.

at Acme Brick Company and in 1982, suggested that Knautz join him at Acme Brick. The company was in the midst of the reorganization following John Justin's taking up the reins of Justin Industries and was in need of a financial officer. Knautz had come to the realization that he wanted to work in the private sector and saw the opportunity to move from public service to private sector manufacturing. In August 1982, he joined Acme Brick Company as controller, with responsibilities for accounting, data processing, and credit. He sat in on the management meetings and worked closely with Ed Stout, Harrold Melton, and John Koch.

He did admit to being somewhat concerned that Acme Brick and Justin Industries were not doing well in 1981 and in the first-half of 1982, but was heartened when Stout explained that "brick is a cyclical business. It's been good, it's been bad, it's going to be good again."[14]

As part of his responsibilities, Knautz worked with the team that was installing BRIX at Acme Brick Company's Fort Worth headquarters in 1983. Knautz said BRIX brought about "a substantial organizational change. It was an order entry system, but it was not integrated. Our general ledger system could not process an order more than $9,999,999."[15]

Bill Lemond, Knautz's former boss at Fort Worth City Transit, was working as Acme Brick Company's planning director when BRIX was developed and installed in the early 1980s. He recalled that when he joined Acme Brick in 1978, the company's offices were typing orders and sending them to different plants every day. "The average time from placing an order to delivering product was ten working days," he said. "I can remember being out in the plants and seeing the dispatcher handwriting orders and shuffling them on a table top."[16]

Although BRIX wasn't integrated with all the company functions, Lemond remembers thinking at the time that Acme Brick had computerized a brick order. He recalled showing Ed Stout a twenty-page computer printout for a brick order and Stout remarking: "We really need to condense this."[17] Still, Lemond credited BRIX with being the company's first step in automating the manufacture and sale of brick. "That automation affects every facet of our business today," he said.[18]

Susan Marvel, who started as a part-time file clerk at Acme Brick Company's Dallas office in 1982, recalled the early BRIX computers with the green screens. "You could hear the little message beep in your sleep," she said.[19] She particularly recalled the dot-matrix daisy wheel printer with its box of paper leading

THE LIFE AND CAREER OF ED STOUT

Edward L. Stout, Jr., was the face of Acme Brick Company to the U.S. brick community for more than a generation. All told, his career at Acme Brick Company spanned the last half of the twentieth century.

Born in Minden, Louisiana, at noon on Thanksgiving Day in 1925, Stout graduated from high school in Ida, Louisiana, in 1943 and immediately volunteered for the U.S. Army Air Corps cadet program. He received his honorable discharge from the service in 1945 and enrolled at Louisiana Tech, where he graduated in 1949 with a degree in mechanical engineering.

Stout had a job lined up in the summer of 1949 with Texas Eastern Pipeline Company when he ran into a high school classmate working for Acme Brick Company who said his boss was trying to hire a mechanical engineering graduate. Stout went and interviewed with the company.

"They offered me $25 a week more than Texas Eastern but agreed to throw in a company car," Stout recalled. "I said, 'I'll take it.'"[1] After spending six weeks in the summer and fall of 1949 undergoing training in Fort Worth, Stout was transferred to the Shreveport, Louisiana, office to serve as a sales engineer, calling on architects. In 1950, he switched to general sales.

"Louisiana only had the Shreveport office," Stout said, "but we had dealers around the state. I worked the northern half of the state, including Monroe and Alexandria. I called on architects and homebuilders."[2]

Selling back then often involved night hours. Stout recalled the time he was trying to sell a more expensive specialty brick to a School Board in Harrisonburg, Louisiana. The chairman of the School Board wanted to personally pick out the brick and invited Stout to meet him at the boat landing in Jonesville, Louisiana. Stout got into a flat-bottom boat with the president, who promptly offered the Acme Brick salesman a drink of whiskey and guided the boat out into the dark swamp. Stout pulled the specialty brick out of his briefcase and showed it to the school official before the light completely faded, who said it looked just fine to him.[3]

In 1959, Stout became the company's Louisiana regional manager and moved to Baton Rouge. Acme Brick Company had acquired brick plants in Louisiana in the early 1950s and had seven distribution yards in the state's major cities.

In 1963, D. O. Tomlin asked Stout to move to corporate headquarters in Fort Worth. It was Thanksgiving weekend, and Stout and his family drove right through downtown Dallas past Dealey Plaza, where President Kennedy had been assassinated the week before. Stout rented a three-bedroom apartment in Fort Worth, and Tomlin, a Harvard MBA, immediately sent Stout to New York City for five weeks of American Management Association training.[4]

Stout spent a little over a year in Fort Worth. In late 1964, he popped into Tomlin's office to tell him that he and his wife had purchased a house in Tarrant County. "There was a dead silence," Stout said. "Tomlin said, 'We want you to move back to Louisiana.'"[5] Tomlin wanted to decentralize Acme Brick Company and set up operating divisions in Texas, Louisiana, Oklahoma, Arkansas, Kansas, and Missouri. Stout helped set up Acme Brick of Louisiana in early 1965, and in 1967 was asked to move to Little Rock to run Acme Brick of Arkansas. Stout returned from a summer 1970 family camping trip to Lake Ouachita in the Ozarks to discover "the phone ringing off the wall. Tomlin, three vice presidents, and eleven board members were all gone."[6] Stout and Vice President Bill Daugherty were the only remaining vice presidents left.

The management upheaval had been engineered by John Justin, who had merged his boot company with Acme Brick Company several years before and folded it into First Worth Company, a corporate holding company. Justin was named president of Acme Brick Company in 1970, and First Worth soon after changed its named to Justin Industries, Inc. Justin named Stout president of Acme Brick Company in 1973, and it was one of the best executive management decisions the Fort Worth business executive ever made. Stout would remain at the helm of Acme Brick Company for the next twenty-six years, guiding it to some of the best performance in the firm's long history. John Justin called Ed Stout "Mr. Brick," and those who were fortunate enough to work with him certainly thought the name fit.

into the tractor feed. "We kept the printer in the closet because it was so noisy," she said.[20]

BRIX would be the mainframe backbone of Acme Brick Company's information technology initiative for nearly twenty years. It would be upgraded at the end of the 1980s with a Unisys 220/402 computer system and eventually replaced by a sophisticated enterprise resource planning (ERP) system early in the twenty-first century. But BRIX helped the company bridge into an automated delivery/invoice system that sped production and reduced customer-billing time.

An Era of Consolidation and Efficiency

Ed Stout realized when he assumed the presidency of Acme Brick Company in 1973 that the company simply had to become more efficient if it wanted to stay independent under the Justin Industries umbrella. Beginning in the late 1970s, the brick industry in the United States began an era of consolidation, often involving the sale of U.S. brick companies to much larger foreign owners. In 1978, Great Britain's Ibstock Ltd. acquired Marion Brick Company, followed by the purchase of Pennsylvania-based Glen Gery Brick Company a year later. British, Australian,

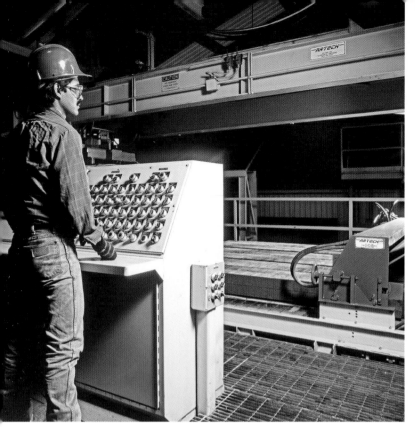

Acme Brick began installing computerized controls at the Denton Plant in the late 1980s.

Brick handling equipment at the Denton Plant became more sophisticated in the late 1980s.

and Canadian brick manufacturers swallowed up American competitors during the 1980s. By 1990, Acme Brick had lost its position as the number one brick manufacturer in the United States. At the time, the company was in third place behind Australian-owned Boral Brick and General Shale, which would be acquired by an Austrian producer in 1999.[21]

One efficiency Acme Brick Company had instituted in the late 1970s and expanded into the 1980s involved transportation. Through the 1950s, as much as 90 percent of the company's brick went to market by rail. But the creation of the nation's Interstate Highway System and the gradual decline of rail passenger and freight traffic set in motion a long-term shift to truck shipment of brick.

By the time the 1980s were underway, Acme Brick was five years into a new concept for shipping brick to customers. In 1975, Justin Industries and Acme had founded Alpha Cargo Motor Express Company (ACME) to utilize owner-operators and company drivers to deliver brick to customers. Between 1976 and 1989, Alpha Cargo took on a greater and greater share of company shipments; during the period, rail shipment dropped from seven thousand cars in 1976 to fewer than one thousand in 1989.[22]

Bill Iams went to work for Alpha Cargo as an owner-operator in 1985. He drove a Peterbilt tractor made at the Denton factory equipped with a boom trailer and worked out of the Bennett Plant. Drivers were allowed to drive ten hours a day, and during peak times, it was not uncommon for Iams to haul as many as

three or four loads a day to local homebuilders. "A lot of times," he said, "the dispatchers would send us out of town, to Sealy or Tulsa. We had sleepers in the cab, so we could live in the truck."[23]

Iams would run loads of brick as far west as Eastern New Mexico and as far east as Missouri and Western Tennessee. "When it slowed in Dallas, they would send us out of town," he said. "There was not a whole lot of deadheading. They tried to keep you loaded."[24]

In the 1980s, Acme Brick becomes the only manufacturer that stamps its name in their brick.

The efficiency of truck transportation dovetailed with the company's increasing marketing efforts during the 1980s. Melton came up with the idea in 1987 of stamping Acme Brick Company's name on the end of residential brick. Harrold Melton focused the company's marketing and promotional efforts on customer relations, and Acme Brick Company embarked in the 1980s upon a decade-long expansion of sales offices in Texas, Louisiana, Kansas, Missouri, Arkansas, and Tennessee.

By 1989, Acme Brick Company had fully weathered the storm clouds of the early 1980s and was looking forward to celebrating its one-hundredth anniversary in 1991. But it would have to endure a bruising takeover battle aimed at wresting control of parent Justin Industries from John Justin.

In the 1980s, Acme Brick marketed "Native Plants" to better identify the company with the states in which it did business, including Oklahoma, Arkansas, and Texas.

CHAPTER 7
THE
CENTENNIAL

1990 TO 1994

In 1991, Acme Brick Company achieved a milestone that eludes all but a few American firms. The company celebrated its centennial anniversary, and took time to reflect on the lessons it had learned since George Bennett incorporated the Acme Pressed Brick Company to operate a plant in the Rock Creek Valley at Bennett, Texas, in the spring of 1891. Acme Brick Company had established a reputation for outstanding customer service, and it was fortunate that it served the rapidly growing market in Texas and the south central United States.

Ed Stout christens an Acme Brick office during the 1991 centennial.

The company was also fortunate in that it had enjoyed stable and visionary leadership during its century of existence. From the family leadership of the Bennetts to the more corporate approach of John Justin, Acme Brick Company had been blessed with leaders who looked beyond the financial results of the next quarter to the health of the long-term marketplace. In 1991, when it celebrated its centennial, Acme Brick Company was in the capable hands of Ed Stout, whose career with the Fort Worth brick company spanned more than half of the company's history. Stout was assisted by industry veterans like Harrold Melton and John Koch, and a workforce that exhibited loyalty and an outstanding work ethic; many of those workers were second- and third-generation team members who could trace their employment back to the Bennett family.

Acme brick inside of a kiln at two thousand degrees.

John Justin arrives on horseback at Acme Brick for the centennial celebration in 1991.

The *Fort Worth Star-Telegram* reported on the Acme Brick Centennial with an interview of Ed Stout in April 1991.

Like any company that instinctively understands the importance of its roots and culture, Acme Brick Company chose to celebrate its centennial by chronicling the company's first one hundred years. During the centennial year, every Acme Brick Company plant and sales office scheduled well-publicized anniversary celebrations. The company hired the Ashley and Taylor public relations team to coordinate the centennial activities at the forty-seven locations in seven states, and Acme Brick Company's marketing department made sure to key the entire year's marketing focus to the one-hundred-year anniversary.[1] Ashley and Taylor provided highlights of the company's first one hundred years of operation to both local media and industry trade journals.

"Acme's original Bennett Plant (designated a Texas historic landmark) continues in full operations today," John Justin told shareholders in early 1991. "It is a tribute to the foresight and wisdom of its founder, George Bennett."[2]

John Justin, Ed Stout, and the Acme Brick Company executive team valued the traditions and culture of the company. To keep that culture alive, the company commissioned a detailed narrative history of Acme Brick Company. As early as 1971, John Justin helped underwrite the research into the history of the Fort Worth–based company by a doctoral student from Texas Christian University. Edwin E. Lehr, Sr., earned his doctorate in 1972 with a dissertation on the history of Acme Brick Company, and in the early 1990s, Lehr was the president of San Jacinto College North. Lehr agreed to update his dissertation, which was published in 1998 by the Donning Company Publishers as *Colossus in Clay: Acme Brick Company, The Story of the Largest American-Owned Brickmaker*.[3] The book would serve as the definitive history of Acme Brick Company for decades and would enhance the company's reputation for preserving its culture.

Entering a Second Century

Acme Brick Company was in a strong position to achieve additional growth as it celebrated its centennial in 1991. The company had shipped just over 555 million brick in 1990, recovering from the 1987 recession when it produced less than 480 million brick. The housing market was sliding into another recession in 1990 and 1991, but Acme Brick Company continued its longtime strategy of investing in the business at a time when housing activity slowed in order to respond quickly when the market began its inevitable recovery. The Justin Industries *1990 Annual Report* noted "through judiciously expanding inventories in markets that hold the greatest recovery potential, the company is poised to substantially increase earnings when the market returns to normal conditions."[4]

Acme Brick Company constituted the bulk of the Building Materials segment of Justin Industries' balance sheet. In 1990, Building Materials reported net sales of $114.2 million, about 36 percent of the parent company's net sales. With profit of just over $3 million, Building Materials accounted for 15 percent of Justin Industries' profit.[5] The company had recovered well from the 1987 recession. Net sales for the Building Material segment had fallen to $105.25 million in 1988, so the 1990 numbers were nearly 10 percent better two years later. And profits in 1990 were six times the $519,000 reported in 1989.[6]

During 1990, Acme Brick Company completed substantial improvements at a number of its sales facilities. Glass block sales

The 1990s centennial celebration advertisement.

increased dramatically late in 1990, thanks to the company's incorporation of a new technique of setting glass block in Innovative Building Products' (IBP) prefabricated metal frames.[7] In 1992, Acme Brick Company would feature the IBP system at its exhibit for the National Association of Homebuilders in Las Vegas, Nevada.

Tell the reindeer this operation's gonna take a while. It's <u>Acme</u> Brick.

Acme Brick's humorous Christmas Card in 1990; the company has sent custom Christmas Cards to customers for twenty-five years.

The increased brick shipments during the year tested Acme Brick Company's transportation system, but the firm was able to bypass some of the bottlenecks with superior customer service and the introduction of centralized trucking coordination. With the installation of a new higher-capacity main frame computer to run its BRIX system, Acme Brick Company's IT Department was able to lower maintenance and utility costs while positioning the company to better respond to increased sales and production volume during the 1990s. Acme Brick Company further enhanced the BRIX system in its centennial year by automating the sample order process, enabling the company's sales office to order brick samples or catalog sheets electronically, thus speeding the response to the customer's need.[8]

Acme Brick Company also paid attention to future needs. Capital expenditure projects during the year included a 50 percent capacity increase at the San Felipe Plant near Houston. The multimillion-dollar expansion was designed to meet market demand for additional product in the booming South Texas area.

The 1990 passage of the federal Clean Air Act amendments made environmental compliance all the more of a priority for brick manufacturers. Acme Brick Company took a proactive approach to the new legislation, maintaining its pace-setting efforts in environmental compliance by installing the first dry scrubber for fluorides abatement in the brickmaking industry in the United States as part of the San Felipe Plant expansion. The company also began work on a wetlands system to provide for water pH control using organic matter as a filtering medium. The system, the first of its kind in the structural clay industry, would benefit the regional ecology and also provide improved wildlife habitat.[9] The company's Central Arkansas Wetlands Project would be completed in 1991 and would set the bar for the industry in the years to come.

By the time it celebrated its centennial year, Acme Brick Company was a valued and growing part of Justin Industries, the parent company. But Justin Industries and its founder, John Justin, had spent all of 1990 in a prolonged proxy fight with outside investors.

The Fight for Justin Industries

John Justin called 1990 "a year of difficult conditions and distractions affecting the company." Justin Industries had reported record sales of nearly $315 million and net income of $7.3 million despite a sharp drop in housing starts and commercial building permits, as well as the uncertainty created by Iraqi dictator Saddam Hussein's invasion of Kuwait.[10] But the year's biggest distraction had come as the result of an attempt

John Justin, seen here in the early 1990s, guided First Worth Corporation for more than thirty years.

by corporate raiders to wrest control of the company from its founder and Board of Directors.

During the summer of 1989, two related investor groups operating under the name of Choctaw Securities and Reatta Partners amassed a 5 percent stake in Justin Industries' stock. The two groups were led by Perry Sutherland, a principal in a chain of Kansas City lumber stores, and Barry Rosenstein, a New York investor who had formerly been associated with corporate raider Asher Edelman. Edelman and the Sutherlands had made a failed attempt earlier in 1989 to take control of Payless Cashways. Rosenstein, a New York investment banker, would go on to become the billionaire founder of Jana Partners, an activist hedge fund. By November, Sutherland and Rosenstein announced they controlled 6.2 percent of the company's stock and intended to initiate a buyout for Justin Industries. At year-end 1990, the group controlled more than 8 percent of Justin Industries stock.[11]

Meanwhile, John Justin was in the process of acquiring the Tony Lama Boot Company for Justin Industries. The company's Board of Directors reappointed the seventy-three-year-old Justin president and CEO for an additional five years, and the Board rejected the buyout offer at its March Annual Meeting of shareholders. In late March 1990, Choctaw and Reatta Partners told the SEC it might file an unfriendly takeover bid for Justin

TROY AIKMAN AND THE ACME BRICK MARKETING CAMPAIGN

Acme Brick Company established itself as one of the more savvy marketers among the nation's brick manufacturers. The company had established a brand recognizable to residents of Texas and the South Central United States during the Mexican brick invasion of the late 1970s and early 1980s and built on that brand awareness during the 1990s with a highly successful advertising campaign featuring Troy Aikman, the Pro Bowl quarterback for the Dallas Cowboys.[1]

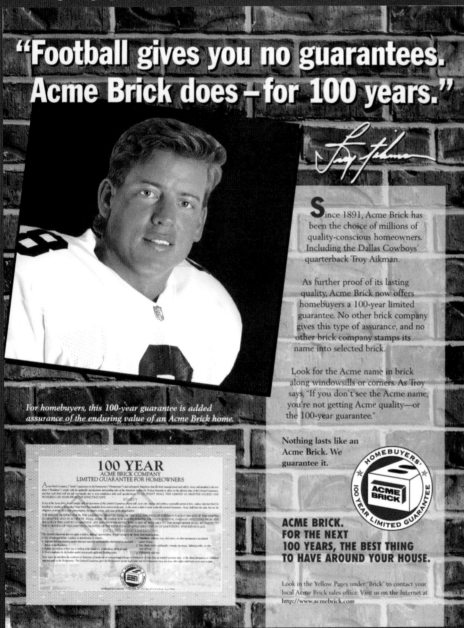

"Football gives you no guarantees. Acme Brick does – for 100 years."

Since 1891, Acme Brick has been the choice of millions of quality-conscious homeowners. Including the Dallas Cowboys' quarterback Troy Aikman.

As further proof of its lasting quality, Acme Brick now offers homebuyers a 100-year limited guarantee. No other brick company gives this type of assurance, and no other brick company stamps its name into selected brick.

Look for the Acme name in brick along windowsills or corners. As Troy says, "If you don't see the Acme name, you're not getting Acme quality—or the 100-year guarantee."

For homebuyers, this 100-year guarantee is added assurance of the enduring value of an Acme Brick home.

Nothing lasts like an Acme Brick. We guarantee it.

ACME BRICK. FOR THE NEXT 100 YEARS, THE BEST THING TO HAVE AROUND YOUR HOUSE.

Look in the Yellow Pages under "Brick" to contact your local Acme Brick sales office. Visit us on the Internet at http://www.acmebrick.com

Dallas Cowboys Quarterback Troy Aikman affirmed the 100-Year Guarantee in 1994.

Aikman was perhaps the most recognized figure in football-mad North Texas while he was the company spokesman. Aikman had taken the Cowboys to Super Bowl victories following both the 1992 and 1993 seasons, and would guide Dallas to a third Super Bowl victory following the 1995 season. His endorsement of Acme Brick Company products provided incalculable benefits to the company. The Aikman endorsement would evolve into a longtime relationship between Acme Brick Company and the Troy Aikman Foundation.[2]

The securing of Aikman as a spokesman, and the generally successful campaign of brand awareness was a result of the hard work of the company's Marketing Department in Fort Worth. Headed by Bill Seidel, the department promoted Acme by having the company named the official brick of the Dallas Cowboys, the Kansas City Chiefs, and the Dallas Mavericks. Seidel, the company's marketing director after 1991, joined Acme Brick Company after earning his MBA from West Texas State University in 1981. He had a background in the construction business before joining Acme Brick Company, and had notable success in raising awareness of Acme Brick and of the company's "quality" story to a very high level among consumers, builders, and architects.[3]

For his efforts at marketing Acme Brick, Seidel received the company's President's Award at the firm's Annual Meeting in 2001.[4]

Industries. Justin Industries filed suit, claiming that Sutherland and Rosenstein were corporate raiders and asking the court to rescind Choctaw's purchases of Justin Industries stock. Sutherland filed a countersuit, asking the court to rescind the March election of Justin Industries directors.[12]

The suits and countersuits were argued throughout the remainder of 1990. Finally, in early 1991, Justin Industries announced it had reached an out-of-court settlement with Choctaw and Reatta Partners. The Fort Worth holding company agreed to pay Sunderland and Rosenstein $1.65 million to avoid any further litigation and to pay legal costs for past litigation. In turn, the two corporate raiders agreed to abandon their hostile takeover attempt and to sell their by then 12 percent stake in Justin Industries to local Texas investors.[13]

At Justin Industries, there was a near palpable sigh of relief the ordeal was over. "The beginning of 1991 saw both positive and negative activity," John Justin told shareholders early in 1992. "Resolution of the attempted hostile takeover of the company was concluded in February; with that unfortunate distraction removed, management and other employees were able to focus their full attention on operating the company."[14]

For Acme Brick Company, although the hostile takeover attempt was peripheral to corporate operations, the end of the yearlong litigation against Justin Industries was welcome news. The parent company was a known commodity, and Justin Industries had owned Acme Brick Company for twenty years, since John Justin merged with the brickmaker in 1971. And if Sutherland and Rosenstein had been successful in their attempt to take control of Justin Industries, they would have likely financed the purchase with debt and may have spun off Acme Brick Company to the highest bidder to help pay off that debt.

Elgin-Butler Brick

After a nearly five-year hiatus from opening new plants or acquiring other brickmakers, Acme Brick Company renewed its commitment to expansion in 1991. It acquired Elgin-Butler Brick Company's Elgin Standard Plant near Austin, Texas. Elgin-Butler, which was located in the heart of Acme Brick Company's direct sales territory, produced both architectural and residential products. Acme Brick Company also acquired the sales rights to Elgin-Butler Brick's line of glazed tile and related products.[15] "The synergies created by this October acquisition promises to put Acme in an even stronger position to serve the Southwestern building materials market," the company said.[16]

Acme Brick Company made employee safety achievements a priority during its centennial year. In 1991, the company recorded a decrease in injuries for the fourth consecutive year. Since the establishment of the Occupational Safety and Health Administration (OSHA) in 1971, Acme Brick Company had made it a corporate strategic goal to reduce workplace injuries and accidents. By 1991, the company's injury frequency rate was less than 10 percent of the national industry average. Still, Acme Brick Company contended with workers' compensation insurance premiums that continued to increase without letup.[17]

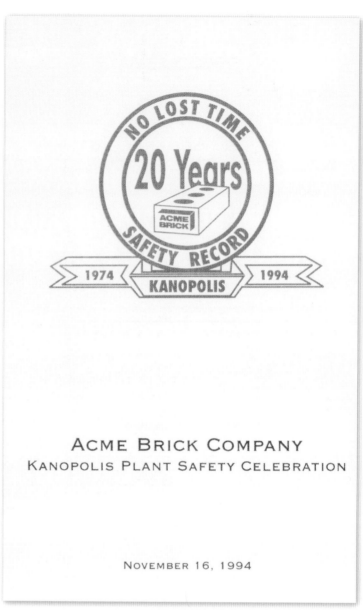

The Kanopolis Plant established a twenty-year safety record with this 1994 No Lost Time Award.

Justin Industries was well pleased with the accomplishments of Acme Brick Company during 1991, a difficult year for the parent company. "Acme Brick Company recorded its ninth consecutive year of market share improvement in 1991," Justin Industries reported in its *1991 Annual Report*. "The company shipped close to an all-time record volume of brick and continued to operate profitably despite enduring the fifth year of severely depressed markets and further declines in the number of housing starts."[18]

Recovering from the Recession

The housing recession that had plagued the administration of President George H. W. Bush began to abate in 1992. By the time Arkansas Governor Bill Clinton captured the White

China Pearl Brick from
the Perla Plant in a 1990s
advertising photo.

House in November 1992, the recession was receding into the rearview mirror of what promised to be a new political and economic environment.

For Acme Brick Company, 1992 was the best year since the early 1980s. The company produced further gains in market share and revenue, breaking sales records previously set in 1984. For the Building Materials group, Acme Brick Company's strong performance contributed to a sales increase of 29 percent in 1991, and operating profits were up a whopping 230 percent. Consolidated net sales at parent company Justin Industries topped $453 million, while the holding company's net income of just over $27 million was triple that reported in 1991.[19]

Acme Brick Company's performance was all the more outstanding considering how widespread it was across all segments of the company's business. At year-end in 1992, Ed Stout reported that MBE shipments set a new monthly record in ten of the twelve months of 1992. "For the year, a new all-time record of 719,932 MBE were delivered to customers, breaking the 1983 mark by 24 percent," Stout said.[20] From a plant perspective, nine plants set all-time shipping marks, including Bridgeport, Elgin, and San Felipe, Texas; Oklahoma City and Tulsa, Oklahoma; Ouachita and Fort Smith, Arkansas; Weir, Kansas; and Dixie, Louisiana.[21] From a sales territory perspective, record annual sales totals were reported from Houston, San Antonio, Austin, and Texarkana, Texas; St. Louis, Springfield, and Joplin, Missouri; and Springdale, Arkansas.[22]

"Based on the records in South Texas," Stout explained, "one can determine that the acquisition of the Elgin Plant as well as the expansion of the San Felipe Plant played major roles in the company's ability to record much higher shipping levels in 1992."[23] Prices during the year jumped an average of 6.3 percent, and purchased product sales continued to set new records. Bagged goods sales were up 20 percent over 1991, while floor and wall tile sales increased by 19 percent year-over-year.[24]

Marketing efforts in 1992 concentrated on an emphasis of the Acme Brick Company logo to remind buyers of the underlying value of the Acme brand. The company also marketed its complete masonry supply centers and invested in a total upgrade of showrooms in Alexandria, Louisiana, and Springdale, Arkansas. Acme Brick Company reinforced its commitment to the industry, playing a leading role in brick marketing councils both locally and nationally; a team of company engineers made presentations to more than two hundred universities and architectural firms on the role that masonry could play in their future construction plans.

Acme Brick was known for having fun with employee presentations; here, John Koch as "General George Patton" and Britt Stokes as his adjutant prepared to talk to the troops in the 1990s.

Under the leadership of John Koch, who was considered one of the best men in U.S. brick production, Acme Brick Company introduced a new concept for clay mining. It developed regional mining plans to fully utilize the increasingly more sophisticated and expensive mining equipment used in the industry. The new mining concept included a change from the use of high-maintenance self-loading scrapers to off-road trucks and large excavators. The company also established new production capabilities at its Tulsa, Oklahoma, Plant that enabled an increase in sales to the growing residential paving market.[25]

Acme Brick Company continued to invest in new computer technology during the year. It added purchased product inventory to the BRIX system and installed a new mainframe disk system that reduced system response time by 48 percent. The IT Department also automated consumer credit requests, eliminating paperwork and reducing response time from as much as a month to less than three days.

Acme Brick Company ended 1992 with a backlog of brick orders that was significantly greater than the backlog at the beginning of the year. The company looked forward to 1993 with renewed enthusiasm.

"A Banner Year"

That optimism was not misplaced. By the time 1993 was in the books, Acme Brick Company and the Building Materials group had led Justin Industries to new records in both sales and earnings. The holding company reported a new high in sales approaching $475 million and in net income of $37.1 million, an increase of 37 percent over 1992.

"Acme posted a banner year due to strong levels of brick shipments and sales of purchased products," John Justin told shareholders, "reflecting residential construction growth in the company's markets, as well as improved pricing coupled with the efficiencies of increased production."[26]

Basketball fans got a chuckle out of this 1993 cartoon linking Acme Brick with poor shooting percentage.

For the year, Acme Brick Company increased its shipment of brick 1 percent to 730 million MBE. Annual shipping records were set in Springfield and Joplin, Missouri; Austin, San Antonio, and Harlingen in South Texas, as well as in Texarkana and plants in Ouachita, Fort Smith, Oklahoma City, Bennett, Elgin, and Garrison. The best news, however, was the company's ability to increase prices. For the year, the average delivered price increased nearly 11 percent from 1992.[27]

Stout reported that purchased product sales for December, the fourth quarter, and all of 1993 were "superb." December sales were up 29 percent over the same period last year. The fourth quarter sales volume set a record for any quarter, exceeding $6 million for the first time. And annual sales set a new high for the fifth consecutive year, this year surpassing the $21 million level. New sales records were set in twenty-three of the thirty-seven sales territories."[28]

The increased shipments and sales, coupled with the company's ability to charge higher prices, created an unprecedented level of profits. "Pretax profits of $2,522,000 were by far the most ever recorded in a December by the company," Stout reported to Justin Industries management. "All-time record net income for the year of $19,087,000 surpassed plan by 56.7 percent and produced a year over year earnings gain of 120 percent."[29]

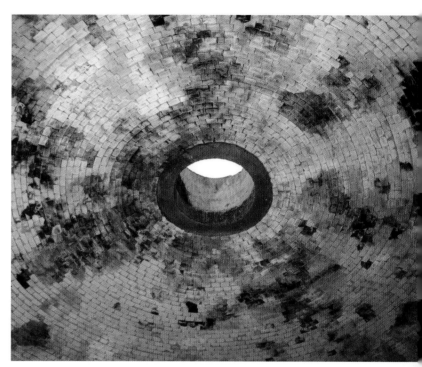

The interior of a beehive kiln, a completely self-supporting structure, is captured in these images.

In the late 1980s and 1990s, Acme began selling more products that the company did not manufacture, like the items pictured above.

As part of its long-term strategy, Acme Brick Company continued to make the capital investments to keep its plants producing in the future. The company upgraded the brick machine at its Fort Smith Plant, relined two kilns at the Bridgeport Plant, completed a kiln car rehabilitation project at the McQueeney Plant, and completed roof repairs at the Denton Plant.[30] One of the larger capital investments completed during the year was the replacement of existing brick extruders at the Denton Plant with the largest machines available.

With a market share in its Texas and South Central U.S. sales territory estimated at more than 50 percent, Acme Brick Company anticipated further gains in 1994. The plan for the year called for the increase of production levels wherever possible and an expansion of the company's purchased products division.

"An Extremely Successful Year"

Acme Brick Company didn't disappoint in 1994. John Justin had expected what he called "another strong year in the Building Materials area, with Acme Brick Company leading the way with its robust market share, and continued growth in purchased products operations. This expectation was certainly borne out by an extremely successful year by Acme Brick. Demand for brick was strong, testing our ability to produce and deliver the record-setting quantities of brick demanded by our customers."[31]

Acme Brick Company sold more than 750 million brick during 1994 to help the Building Materials group record a 25 percent increase in revenues and a 42 percent gain in operating profits. Acme Brick Company's purchased products division continued to excel, increasing sales almost 20 percent from 1993. Sales in the division were accelerated in August when Acme Brick Company closed on the purchase of American Tile

100 YEAR
ACME BRICK COMPANY
LIMITED GUARANTEE FOR HOMEOWNERS

Acme Brick Company ("Acme") guarantees to the homeowner ("Homeowner") and subsequent transferees that the brick manufactured and sold by Acme and installed in the residence ("Residence") comply with the applicable specifications and grading rules of the American Society for Testing Materials in effect on the effective date of this Limited Guarantee, and that such brick will not fail structurally due to non-compliance with such specifications. IN NO EVENT SHALL THIS LIMITED GUARANTEE EXCEED ONE HUNDRED (100) YEARS FROM THE EFFECTIVE DATE.

REMEDY

If any of the Acme brick do not comply with the provisions of this Limited Guarantee, Acme will, at its sole expense and within a reasonable period of time, replace defective brick by installing or causing to be installed Acme brick then available from current production. In the event a claim is made under this Limited Guarantee, Acme shall have the right, but not the obligation, to verify, by its own representative, the nature, extent, and cause of the alleged defect.

THE REMEDY PROVIDED FOR IN THIS LIMITED GUARANTEE SHALL BE THE SOLE AND EXCLUSIVE REMEDY FOR ANY BREACH OF THIS LIMITED GUARANTEE, AND IN NO EVENT SHALL ACME BE LIABLE FOR ANY INCIDENTAL OR CONSEQUENTIAL DAMAGES RESULTING FROM ANY BREACH OF THIS LIMITED GUARANTEE. ANY IMPLIED WARRANTIES WHICH MAY BE AVAILABLE TO THE HOMEOWNER SHALL BE LIMITED TO THE DURATION OF THIS LIMITED GUARANTEE OR THE EXPIRATION OF APPLICABLE STATUES OF LIMITATIONS, WHICHEVER IS LESS.

EXCLUSIONS AND LIMITATIONS

This Limited Guarantee does not apply to failure, damage, deterioration, or color change to the Acme brick resulting from:

a. Use of improper mortar or failure or deterioration of mortar;

b. Improper building practices and/or improper masonry workmanship which result in structural defects in the Residence;

c. Failure or cracking of brick due to settling of the Residence or subsidence of the ground;

d. Non-compliance by the builder and/or mason with applicable building codes;

e. Vandalism, collision, war, civil unrest, or other intentional or accidental events or acts;

f. Fire, flood, storm, earthquake, tornado, hurricane, lightning strike, or other Acts of God;

g. Pollution or acid rain.

Some states do not allow the exclusion or limitation of incidental or consequential damages or limitations on how long an implied warranty lasts, so the above limitations or exclusions may not apply to the Homeowner. This Limited Guarantee gives the Homeowner specific legal rights and the Homeowner may also have other rights which vary from state to state.

ACME BRICK COMPANY   P.O. Box 425 • Fort Worth, Texas 76101

Acme Brick instituted the "100 Year Limited Guarantee" in 1994, a first for the industry.

Supply Company (ATS), one of the nation's largest independent distributors of ceramic and marble floor tile.[32] The sale, which closed for $16 million, gave Acme Brick Company a new tool to use in its strategy to strengthen its purchased products line. John Justin characterized prospects for future growth of the new acquisition as "excellent."[33]

The company was also in the midst of a second major brick expansion in just the past five years. In 1994, Acme Brick Company signed contracts for the construction of a new, state-of-the-art brick manufacturing facility at Bennett, Texas, the site where George Bennett had begun making brick just over a century before. The new plant was slated to expand the company's brickmaking capacity by 8 percent and would boast the best available technology and environmental controls.[34]

With construction well underway on the new Bennett Plant in 1995, Acme Brick Company was positioning itself to meet demand in the rapidly approaching twenty-first century.

CHAPTER 8
INTO A NEW CENTURY
1995 TO 1999

From a print ad for Innovative Building Products in 1998; Acme Brick sold the vault ceiling.

Acme Brick Company emerged in the mid- to late 1990s as a dynamic driver of the residential and commercial real estate boom sweeping Texas and the Southwest. The company returned to its strategy of acquisition through growth, buying Fort Worth–based Innovative Building Products in 1997, the developer and manufacturer of a mortarless installation system for glass block windows, skylights, shower enclosures, and floors. Acme Brick Company followed the 1997 acquisition with the 1998 acquisition of Witt Brick & Supply, which became the company's Temple, Texas sales facility. Witt, one of Acme Brick Company's fiercest competitors, was subsequently skillfully integrated into the Acme Brick Company culture. The company's acquisition of the two Texas Clay Brick Plants in Malakoff further grew Acme Brick Company's core business.

The company also made provisions for its raw material needs for the future; Acme Brick Company focused on the acquisition of clay reserves in Texas and the Southwest during the period surrounding the turn of the twenty-first century.

Acme Brick was also the official brick of the Kansas City Chiefs in 1998.

THE LIFE AND CAREER OF HARROLD MELTON

When Ed Stout stepped down as president of Acme Brick Company in 1999, Harrold Melton thought it was a fairly good bet that Stout's replacement would be one of the company's senior executives. At the time, Stout's executive team consisted of Melton, the vice president of marketing; John Koch, the vice president of operations; and Dennis Knautz, the vice president of finance and CFO.

Melton was "pleased and not totally surprised" when he was selected to succeed Stout. "I was pretty sure that the next president would be an insider, so I had a 33 percent chance."[1]

At the time he was named Acme Brick Company's new president, Melton was sixty-three years old and a twenty-five-year veteran with the Fort Worth brickmaker. He would skillfully guide Acme Brick Company into the twenty-first century, and would help negotiate the sale of the company to Warren Buffett and Berkshire Hathaway in 2001. He would cap his thirty-six-year career with Acme Brick Company in his retirement year of 2005 when he was recognized with the Brick Industry Association's Outstanding Achievement Award.[2] "I was elated that my peers in the brick industry felt well enough about me to select me for the BIA Award," Melton said in a 2014 interview.[3]

A Different Career Path

Born in Northeastern Oklahoma during the Dust Bowl years of the mid-1930s, Harrold Melton followed a different career path to the pinnacle of Acme Brick Company. When Melton was sixteen, his father died in a tragic accident while helping a local Rural Electrification Administration crew, and the family moved across Oklahoma to Guymon, where he graduated from high school. He enrolled at Panhandle State College, married Betty, his high school sweetheart, and dropped out after one semester to support his family. After working at a supermarket chain and as a salesman for George A. Hormel for several years, he accepted a job with Acme Brick Company in 1958. Acme assigned him to a sales territory covering Western Oklahoma and Western Kansas, and Harrold and Betty Melton moved to Liberal, Kansas.[4] In 1959 at a regional sales meeting in Oklahoma City, Melton met Ed Stout, then the Louisiana regional sales manager.[5]

About a year later, Stout called Melton and offered him the job as district manager in Monroe, Louisiana. Harrold and Betty Melton, and their two children moved to Louisiana, and he would be one of Stout's top salesmen for the next four years. But ever since dropping out of college, Harrold and Betty had dreamed of going back to school to get their college degrees. In 1964, Melton wrote Stout to tell him that he and Betty had enrolled at the University of Oklahoma in Norman. Stout quickly arranged for Melton to transfer to Acme Brick Company's sales office, and Melton continued working for the company while attending classes; when Betty Melton earned her B.S. degree in elementary education in 1966, Stout asked the Meltons to move to Baton Rouge where Harrold could complete his degree work at Louisiana State University and continue working for Acme Brick Company.[6]

Melton completed his B.S. in business in the spring of 1967. "As things turned out," he said, "I didn't find an Acme opening that was a good fit for me." Melton left Acme Brick Company in early 1968 and completed his MBA at LSU in the summer of 1969. In the fall, he began work on his PhD in finance at LSU. With all of his coursework completed in the late summer of 1970, Melton accepted a faculty position at West Texas State University in Canyon. He completed his dissertation, took final exams at LSU in 1973, and was awarded his doctorate in 1974.

Harrold Melton might had gone on to a long and distinguished career in academia, but Ed Stout, by then president of Acme Brick Company, had never forgotten just how good a salesman Harrold Melton was. In 1975, he contacted Melton with an offer to return to Acme Brick Company. Melton accepted and was eager to return home.[7]

Building A Sales Team

In July of 1975, Melton returned to Acme Brick Company as regional sales manager of an area that included Dallas–Fort Worth, one of the largest brick markets in the nation. He quickly realized that the industry was under assault from a very serious threat—under-fired "adobe brick" imported from Mexico. Estimates of yearly shipments of these poor quality brick during this time approached 500 million, and Mexican brick's market share in Texas, the largest brick consuming state in the country, was estimated to be 50 percent. As a result, Mexican brick had been a contributing factor in the closure of seventeen brick plants in Texas during the previous ten years.

The battle against substandard, low-priced Mexican brick was long and hard, but Acme Brick Company and the industry were able to decrease the demand for poor quality brick and increase non-Mexican brick's market share dramatically. Estimates of Mexican brick sales were below 10 percent in Texas by the mid-1980s. An additional outcome attributable to Melton's leadership of the industry was that homeowners throughout Texas received high quality clay brick on their homes instead of a product that consistently failed over time. It was an important battle in Acme Brick Company's history, and a story that will perhaps never be completely told. Harrold Melton became visibly identified with the battle against Mexican brick early on, and put his job on the line in the process. But that willingness to risk everything was how Melton handled adversity.

In 1977, Melton was named general sales manager and assumed responsibility for Acme Brick Company's entire sales effort. He began building a sales team that would provide Acme's customers with superior service and quality products at a fair price. Melton believed that to attain the goal of complete customer satisfaction, Acme Brick Company must build and maintain an ethical, customer-oriented organization comprised of honorable, trusted employees.

In 1981, Acme Brick Company created a new position within the company, naming Melton as vice president of sales. At the time, he was promoted to the position, Melton was the company's only vice president. Melton quickly expanded Acme's Technical Service Department to include four engineers. During the 1980s and 1990s, the Technical Service Department devoted untold hours to the development of educational programs presented to architectural firms and to architectural and engineering students at major colleges and universities.

Melton also oversaw the company's Marketing Department, which worked tirelessly to establish Acme Brick Company's brand in the Texas and South Central U.S. markets. In the 1990s, the use of Dallas Cowboys quarterback Troy Aikman as a spokesman for the company created unbelievable name recognition and goodwill for Acme Brick Company. In May 1995, Melton spearheaded Acme Brick Company's introduction of a 100-year guarantee. The guarantee was eventually adopted by almost all the major manufacturers in the brick industry and helped position clay brick nationwide as a superior product compared to less durable cladding materials.[8] He also approved the purchase of brick.com at a great price.

"Strategies That Resulted in Success"

For a quarter-century, Ed Stout and Harrold Melton defined excellence in the nation's brick industry. When Stout retired in 1999, it was really no great surprise that the Justin Industries Board of Directors chose Harrold Melton to replace his old friend and mentor. And Melton would not disappoint the trust placed in him. During his tenure as president and CEO, Melton would guide the company through an organizational change that combined Acme Brick Company and Featherlite Building Products to form a single organization. He was also very instrumental in the acquisition of Acme Brick Company by Berkshire Hathaway.

Looking back, Melton said his accomplishments included improved profitability, customer recognition of the Acme brand, and improved sales of brick and purchased products. "Sales group stability improved over time, and sales group performance improved," Melton said. "And, Acme delivered to customers more than 1 billion brick for the first time ever."[9]

But Melton was quick to note that he could not have done it all alone. "Most credit for the accomplishments above should go to Acme employees who executed strategies that resulted in success," he pointed out.[10]

Paying Tribute to the Past

On a Friday evening in early November 1996, Acme Brick Company paid tribute to its past—and to its future. At a gala plant tour and Texas barbecue, the company unveiled its new state-of-the-art brick manufacturing plant at Bennett, Texas. Located just a few hundred yards from the site of the company's original plant established in 1891 by George Ellis Bennett, the new plant boasted a 552-foot-long tunnel, or continuous kiln. The longest gas-fired kiln in the United States, it gave the new Bennett Plant the capacity of producing more than 1 million King Size Brick each week.[1]

Tour guides that Friday evening explained to the nearly 750 customers, employees, Justin Industries officials, and friends of Acme Brick Company that the new plant would produce brick in deep red, shades of plum, charcoal, and gray. They noted that

Texas Rangers slugger Juan Gonzalez at the House that Juan Built, a charitable partnership with Acme Brick and Habitat for Humanity.

drying the new kiln and bringing it to operating temperatures took more than a month, and much of the spring and summer of 1996 was spent adjusting the new kiln to characteristics of Bennett's clays.[2]

The new plant represented the largest single investment in Acme Brick Company's long history, but it was one that the company felt more than justified in making. "We see an ever-increasing appreciation for the qualities that hard-fired brick bring to a project," Company President Ed Stout told the crowd.[3] He also noted that with the addition of the new Bennett Plant, Acme Brick Company would offer the broadest variety of quality brick products in the company's history.

The new Bennett Plant came on-line at an opportune time. Acme Brick Company established new records for sale of brick and purchased products in 1996, with revenues increasing 9 percent to a record high in Justin Industries' building materials group. Higher natural gas prices and the start-up costs associated with the new Bennett Plant kept profits at a level slightly below the record year of 1994.[4]

What drove Acme Brick Company's very solid 1996 numbers was the continuing performance of the Texas and South Central U.S. housing market. The company sold 12 percent more brick in 1996 than it had in 1995, despite earlier predictions of a drop in housing starts by the mid-1990s. "Forecasters had predicted that the rate of housing starts would fall as the aging baby boom generation was replaced by a much smaller population group," Justin Industries explained in its *1996 Annual Report*. "This has not occurred nationally, and particularly in Acme's home territory, for two major reasons. First, immigration and migration is at the highest level in the 1990s since the turn of the century; and second, the highest percentage of home ownership is found among the country's older population (those over sixty-five), with this age group

Troy Aikman with legendary pro football player and broadcaster Pat Summerall.

Acme Brick supported Super Bowl winning Quarterback Troy Aikman and his Foundation throughout the 1990s.

Pat Summerall doing radio advertisements for Acme Brick in the 1990s.

Sports Illustrated

Above: Troy Aikman enjoyed hands-on experiences when visiting Acme Brick facilities.

Left: Acme Brick created a special promotion with *Sports Illustrated* when it celebrated its 105th birthday in 1996.

growing rapidly. So far in the 1990s, these factors have created a stronger demand than anticipated."[5]

Acme Brick Company capitalized on that stronger than anticipated demand by concentrating its advertising and marketing focus on reinforcing the company's brand awareness, while promoting the 100-year limited guarantee for homeowners and the company's 105-year reputation for quality.

In 1996, Acme Brick Company sent a series of monthly mailings to more than seven thousand architects in the company's sales territory. The mailings promoted the beauty, strength, and versatility of Acme Brick, reinforcing the reality of Acme Brick as the building material of preference in Texas and the South Central U.S.[6]

As part of its strategic plan to increase the sale of brick, Acme Brick Company continued to improve its distribution network by adding new sales offices and expanding existing locations. In 1996, the company completed or started construction of new showrooms, warehouses, and sales offices in Lubbock, Midland, and Corpus Christi, Texas; Little Rock and Fort Smith, Arkansas; and Monroe, Louisiana.[7]

The company also continued to invest in increasing sales of its line of purchased products. American Tile Supply Company, acquired two years previously, reported all-time high sales in 1996 as the per capita use of ceramic tile increased in both Texas and the United States. Acme Brick Company broke ground in 1996 on a third Houston location for its ceramic tile subsidiary and began work on a new warehouse for the firm in Little Rock.[8]

Expanding through Acquisitions

Acme Brick Company's strategic plan for the latter half of the 1990s also called for a continuation of the company's renewed hunt for acquisitions.

The company beefed up its manufacturing capacity in 1998 when it closed on the acquisition of Texas Clay and their two manufacturing plants near Malakoff, Texas. The firm, which had been in business for more than a half-century, was the brickmaking division of Temtex Industries since 1971. Part of the acquisition called for Acme Brick Company to assume Texas Clay's existing backlog. Texas Clay sold primarily to distributors; as a result, all of the orders were booked at dealer prices, a substantial discount to residential pricing that took Acme Brick Company much of 1998 to work through.[9] But the Texas Clay acquisition also brought the company valuable clay deposits southeast of the Dallas–Fort Worth Metroplex.

One Billion Brick

On the last business day of 1999, Acme Brick Company's one-billionth brick produced during calendar 1999 arrived at a David Weekley Home under construction at the Spicewood at Bull Creek development in Austin, Texas. It was the first time in the company's 108-year history that Acme Brick Company had sold and delivered one billion brick in a single year.[10]

The 1 billionth brick had been produced at the company's Garrison, Texas Plant and was part of a batch of blend number 145, "Country French."[11] It arrived in a standard shipment to the Weekley building site but was quickly retrieved by Acme's Austin District Manager Shawn McElroy for the company's collection wall of distinguished brick from around the world at the Fort Worth headquarters. Acme President Harrold Melton said that the accomplishment was "a tribute both to the thriving national economy and to the dedication and work ethic of Acme's 2,156 employees."[12]

Acme closed out the twentieth century with a record-setting year. Brick shipments were up 11 percent over budgeted plan figures, while sales for brick were up 25 percent over 1998, and up 13 percent for purchased products. The company went into the new millennium with a backlog of brick orders equal to approximately five months' shipments. "With brick pricing at record levels," reported President Harrold Melton, "sales and profit expectations for brick products remain high going into 2000."[13]

Employees celebrated Acme Brick's 108th birthday in 1999; in this shot taken from the roof of the headquarters building, John Justin is at bottom of the number 1 with his walker; Harrold Melton is to the left of Justin, and Ed Stout is to Justin's right.

In this 1999 Innovative Building Products installation at LeBonheur Childrens' Hospital in Memphis, Tennessee, lighting beneath the IBP floor system gives the appearance of water rippling underneath the glass pavers.

The Kanopolis Plant in Kansas receives a Safety Award in 1999, four years after it became the only Acme plant to ever win the President's Award in 1995.

Acme Brick furnished the limestone from its Texas Quarries for the exterior of the Bass Performance Hall in Fort Worth in 1998.

Acme Brick Company's strong performance during the latter 1990s did not pass unnoticed by Justin Industries, the parent company. On July 1, 1999, Justin Industries announced that as part of its strategic plan, it was restructuring the company into two operating divisions: footwear and building materials. Justin Industries' approaching sale necessitated Acme Brick taking control of the Building Products Division, which would be consolidated under Acme Brick Company management and would consist of Acme Brick Company, American Tile Supply Company, Featherlite Building Products Corporation, Texas Quarries, and Innovative Building Products, Inc. The new company would be headed by Harrold Melton; Corky Moss, the president of Featherlite Building Products, was named senior vice president of corporate development at Acme Brick Company, reporting to Melton and responsible for integrating the various business units into the new company.[14]

The Passing of the Torch

In April 1999, John Justin became chairman emeritus of the Justin Industries Board. Justin, who had helped grow Acme Brick Company since first becoming acquainted with the firm more than thirty years before, was succeeded as president and CEO of Justin Industries by J. T. Dickenson, a twenty-five-year veteran of the holding company. John V. Roach, the CEO of Tandy Corporation for much of the 1980s and 1990s, succeeded Justin as chairman of the Board of Justin Industries.

Justin's retirement from day-to-day management of Justin Industries was followed two months later by an equally important departure for Acme Brick Company. On June 20, 1999, Ed Stout celebrated fifty years in the clay brick industry with Acme Brick Company. He had retired as president of the company on March 1, 1999, but had agreed to serve as CEO through mid-summer in order to give his replacement, Harrold Melton, time to transition his sales and marketing duties to his replacement.

"It has been fifty years marked by a commitment to excellence, a love of challenges, and a reputation for tackling those challenges head on with inspirational leadership and creative problem solving," Acme Brick Company said in bidding their longtime chief executive goodbye.[15]

Stout began his career with Acme Brick Company as an engineer at the Shreveport office upon graduating from Louisiana Tech University with a B.S. in mechanical engineering in 1949. During the next twenty-four years, he rose through the company's ranks and continually became more involved in Acme's sales efforts. Stout was named field sales manager for Texas, Louisiana, and New Mexico in 1963, and became vice president of Acme Brick Company in 1965. In 1973, Stout was named president of Acme Brick Company by John Justin.[16]

When Ed Stout joined Acme Brick in 1949, company sales were $8 million. In 1998, Acme sales set an all-time company record, achieving sales of $200 million. But Stout's interest in the cause of quality building materials extended well beyond Acme Brick Company. In the late 1980s, Stout had led an effort to develop a national brick industry marketing program. When the effort was ultimately unsuccessful, he urged the development of local brick marketing councils. As a result of his efforts there were thirty local brick marketing councils at work in 1999, spending nearly $6 million annually promoting the use of brick. Nelson Cooney, President of the Brick Industry Association, noted that, "more than anyone else, Ed Stout has furthered the cause of the brick industry."[17]

Stout and his wife, Mitzi, looked forward to spending much of their free time on their two most passionate interests, their family and their love of the outdoors.

Ed Stout left behind big shoes to fill. In the years ahead, Harrold Melton, his successor, would take some giant steps in those big shoes.

Ed Stout in the late 1990s, closing in on nearly a half-century with Acme Brick.

An Acme Brick exploration team in 1998 doing core sampling on company-owned land near the Dixie Plant in Louisiana.

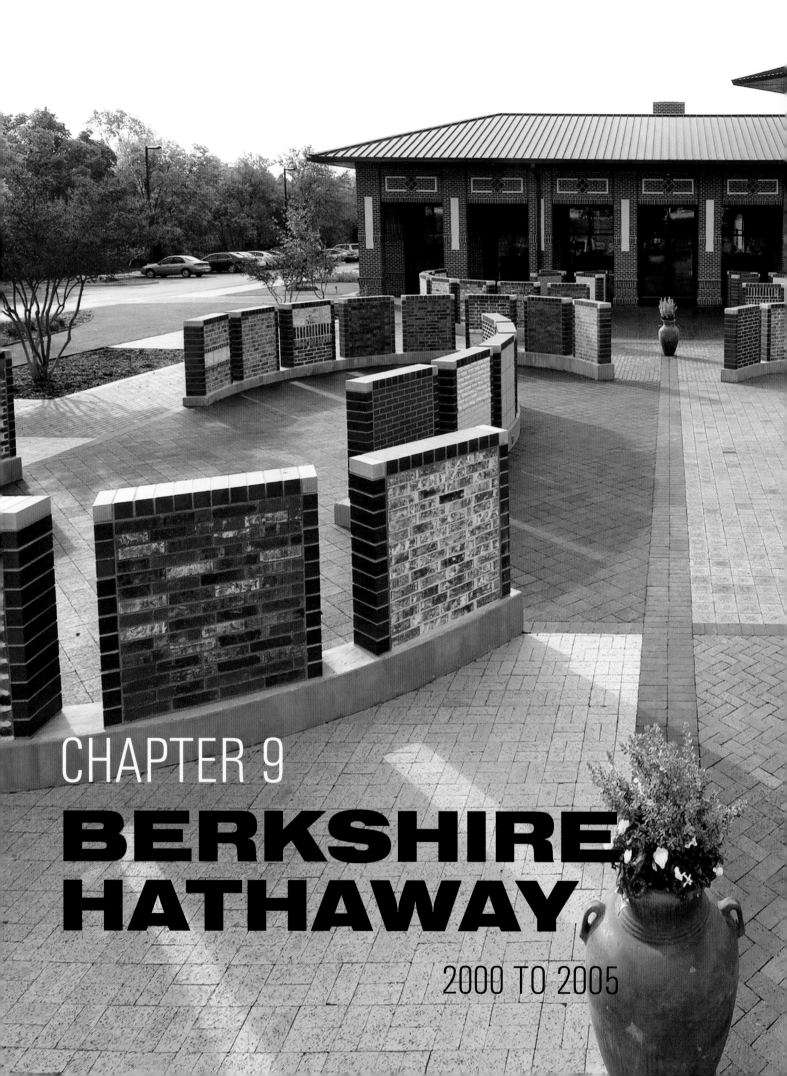

CHAPTER 9
BERKSHIRE HATHAWAY

2000 TO 2005

Harrold Melton strikes a jaunty pose in 2002.

Acme Brick Company's expansion continued in early 2000, including the acquisition of Eureka Brick Company in Clarksville, Arkansas, the acquisition of Wheeler Brick Company in Jonesboro, Arkansas, and the beginning of production at the company's new Elgin, Texas, Handmades Plant. But the 2000 expansion was overshadowed when Omaha investor Warren Buffett's Berkshire Hathaway Group first took an interest in acquiring control of Justin Industries. That summer, Buffett visited Fort Worth, and the Berkshire Hathaway chairman quickly negotiated an acquisition of the Fort Worth conglomerate. Buffett installed his hands-off management style, and Berkshire Hathaway left Harrold Melton in place as president of Acme Brick because of his successful and profitable business practices.

Acme Brick Company continued its expansion policies in the early years of the twenty-first century, after exceeding shipments of 1 billion brick for the first time in 2001. The

Acme Brick's Dallas/Fort Worth Sales Office with its unique brick garden in 2005.

The Betenbough Homes corporate office in Lubbock was built with Acme Brick inside and out.

Costumed reenactors help a young guest make a Colonial Brick at the opening of the Elgin Handmades Plant in 2000.

The management team assists at the ribbon cutting at Acme Brick's Elgin Handmades Plant in 2000.

WARREN BUFFETT: THE ORACLE OF OMAHA

Warren Buffett's decision to add Acme Brick Company to his Berkshire Hathaway portfolio was typical of the Omaha investor's approach to acquisitions. He has often reiterated that his investment strategy is based on the philosophy of only investing in companies and products that the average person can understand.

And Warren Buffett understood brick. Describing his first meeting with Acme Brick Company President and CEO Harrold Melton, Buffett noted that "when Harrold and I first met, he talked about how a home is the largest single investment made by most families. I must say, that like most people, I took the beauty and permanence of my brick home, purchased in 1958, for granted. Then I realized that my total expenditure in maintaining the brick exterior of my home for forty-two years was zero! How many thousands of dollars would I have spent maintaining another type of exterior during the ensuing four decades? Early in my business career, that money spent on maintenance would have been unavailable to invest in quality stocks and companies."[1]

Buffett went on to say that "this incredible value that brick delivers has made Acme a household name in their primary market. We place a high value on investing in companies like these with strong brand positions in their markets like Coke, Gillette, GEICO, and American Express. We know that these companies achieve strong brand preference by consistently delivering superior products, service, and value."[2]

Born in Omaha, Nebraska, in 1930, Buffett became known for his philosophy of value investing that made him one of the nation's richest people. But he was equally well known for his frugality and laid-back Midwestern lifestyle in spite of his great wealth. Buffett is also known for his philanthropic activities, and his oft-stated pledge to give away the vast bulk of his fortune.

The son of a U.S. Congressman from Nebraska, Buffett attended grade school in Washington, D.C., and graduated from Woodrow Wilson High School in the nation's capital. A University of Nebraska graduate, Buffett worked in his hometown of Omaha as an investment salesman, a securities analyst, and a stockbroker after earning his MS in economics from the Columbia Business School in 1951. He made his first million by 1962, and acquired Berkshire Hathaway, a failing textile manufacturing firm, in 1965. By 1990, Buffett's use of Berkshire Hathaway as a holding company to acquire other firms had made the Omaha investor a billionaire.

Buffett's management style was to put good people in place and let them do their jobs. Harrold Melton, who worked with Buffett after the acquisition, considered him "a terrific boss. He grasped the essence of our business immediately, and he never interfered with my operation of Acme. He was normally available by phone when I had a reason to contact him, and he was always gracious and helpful."[3]

Dennis Knautz described Buffett's approach as "pretty much a hands-off management style. At first, we didn't know what the rules were, especially for financial reporting. But we quickly learned to send the reports to Omaha instead of downstairs to Mr. Justin. It was pretty autonomous. Mr. Buffett told us we could call him every day."[4]

company acquired brick plants in Mississippi and Colorado in 2001. Acme Brick acquired distributors Angelo Brick in San Angelo, Texas, and Edmond Materials in Memphis and Jackson, Tennessee, in 2003 and 2005. Acme Brick Company replaced the aging BRIX system in 2004 with a comprehensive ERP solution from J. D. Edwards. The first five years of the twenty-first century concluded with the 2005 retirement of Harrold Melton and his succession as president by Dennis Knautz, a twenty-three-year veteran of the company. All in all, it had been a very productive start of the twenty-first century for Acme Brick Company.

Arkansas Expansion

Acme Brick Company entered the twenty-first century in a strongly expansionist mode. The company had spent the latter half of the 1990s acquiring brick companies in the region and expanding its manufacturing capacity, especially in Texas. In 2000, Acme Brick Company cast its eyes on expansion opportunities in neighboring Arkansas.

Arkansas was a net exporter of brick. The state had extensive, rich clay deposits, and a population of only 2.5 million people. The state had long exported brick to the Metroplex and the rest of Texas, as well as to wholesale and retail customers in Oklahoma and Missouri. Brick manufacturers in the state even exported product to national accounts.

Acme Brick Company had a strong presence in the Razorback State. The company's Perla East, Perla West, and Ouachita Plants were all among Acme Brick Company's best producers. The Perla Plants were known for their White Brick, and the Ouachita Plant was a major producer of residential brick. The Fort Smith Plant had operated an older round kiln that made a very unique brick.

The Ballpark at Arlington accounted for more than 1 million Ranger Red Brick in 2003.

A 2000 International Truck from Acme Brick's Malvern Plant in Arkansas.

David Michie, a Fort Worth native who had started work at Acme Brick Company's Denton Plant while finishing college courses in 1985, moved to Malvern as Central Arkansas regional manager in 1998. Michie was impressed by the work ethic of the brickmakers he encountered at his new assignment. "You've got good strong brickmakers there," Michie said.[1]

Those "good strong brickmakers" were what attracted Acme Brick Company to further Arkansas expansion. In 2000, the company made two acquisitions in the state, Eureka Brick at Clarksville, and Wheeler Brick Company in Jonesboro. The company spent much of 2000 integrating the new acquisitions into its system.

In June 1999, Acme Brick Company had taken possession of Eureka Brick Company of Clarksville, Arkansas. Located in the state's northwestern corner, the fifty-two-year-old Eureka Brick produced a unique brick in a variety of deep red colors that were prized by residential and commercial builders.

When he retired, Ed Stout was retained as a consultant to assist with the purchase of brick plants. "I got to know everybody in the brick business," he said.[2] One of the brick plants Stout was trying to buy for Acme Brick Company was A. J. Johnson's Eureka Brick Company. He and Johnson had gotten to be good friends, but when Johnson died, his wife, Norma, took over ownership of the company. "I had never negotiated with a ghost before," Stout explained. "We eventually paid the widow what A. J. Johnson thought that plant was worth."[3]

The Perla Brick used in the construction of the United Methodist Church in Fort Worth shone as bright in 2005 as when it was installed in the 1930s.

The price was worth it to help Acme Brick Company solidify its dominance of the Arkansas market. "The Eureka Brick and Texas Clay purchases will add 12 percent to our productive capacity and help us meet our customers' demands for Acme brick," Ed Stout told employees. "Further, these operations have ample clay reserves so they can operate for many years before further clay exploration will be required."[4]

Acme Brick Company began negotiations in late 1999 for another major acquisition based in Arkansas: Wheeler Brick Company in Jonesboro, Arkansas. Founded by Ellis R. Wheeler in 1946, the privately held Wheeler Brick Company served markets in Northeastern Arkansas, Southeastern Missouri, and Southwestern Tennessee. The company's Jonesboro, Arkansas plant had a capacity of 35 million brick per year.

Harrold Melton, Acme Brick Company's president and CEO, told the media that "while this acquisition will help by adding about 3 percent to our annual productive capacity, its location will also allow us to support our growing presence in the Memphis area as well as Northeast Arkansas and Southeast Missouri."[5]

Glacier White Brick from Perla shines in this 2005 calendar shot.

Warren Buffett with Betty Melton (left) and Mitzi Stout (right) in 2000.

Mr. Buffett Comes to Town

Acme Brick Company's contribution to the bottom line at Justin Industries had not gone unnoticed by the nation's financial community. In summer of 2000, one of the country's most respected investors gave his seal of approval to Acme Brick Company.

Warren Buffett, "The Oracle of Omaha," had established a reputation as one of America's savviest investors. In the 1990s, Buffett's Berkshire Hathaway holding company had compiled an enviable record by investing in such blue chip stocks as Coca-Cola, Disney, American Express, and Gillette. His investment philosophy involved buying companies he considered "understandable," companies with a simple business model and a long history of successful operation.[6]

Buffett's interest in Acme Brick Company was driven by John Justin's desire to cash out of the holding company he had built over a quarter-century of hard work and shrewd acquisitions. Justin Industries had begun preparing the company's sale in 1999, when Justin stepped down as chairman of the company he had founded. The vast bulk of Justin's fortune was tied up in Justin Industries stock, and Justin had begun to experience health issues in the late 1990s. In essence, Justin had instructed his attorneys to prepare a sale of the company in order to settle his estate.

"John was in a wheelchair at the end," recalled Harrold Melton. "In his last days at the company, he used a walker to get around the office."[7]

As word got out that Justin Industries might be for sale, the company's Board of Directors fielded several queries in early 2000 from the three big brick manufacturers in North America. John Roach, who had grown Radio Shack as the CEO of Tandy Industries, was head of the Justin Industries Board of Directors in 2000. Roach was assisted by J. T. Dickenson, the president and CEO of Justin Industries; Randy Watson, the president and CEO of the Boot and Footwear Division; Melton, president and CEO of the Building Products Division; and Justin Industries' Richard J. Savitz.

Melton and Roach got along well together. A hard-nosed businessman, Roach was "strictly business, and had been around Justin Industries for a long time. I liked him. He liked me."[8]

As Melton recalled, Jeff Bodley, Acme Brick Company's in-house attorney, had a friend in New York who called Buffett and told him that Justin Industries was in play. Justin Industries was already working with the New York investment firm of Donaldson, Lufkin, and Jenrette, because the firm was prepared to deal with proposals to buy Acme Brick Company. Buffett called Roach and scheduled a visit to Fort Worth.

When Buffett got interested in Acme Brick Company, he called his old friend, Bill Gates. The Microsoft chairman's wife was a Dallas native, and she quickly told Buffett that everybody in Dallas knew Acme Brick Company.[9]

Buffett spent most of a June afternoon with Melton, after spending the morning with Randy Watson of the Boot and Footwear Division. Melton explained to Buffett who did what at Acme Brick Company, and outlined the company's operations and future prospects. Before Buffett left that day, he told Roach that he had seen all he needed to see. He added that he didn't buy businesses that needed to be fixed.[10]

Fort Worth landmark Thistle Hill was built in 1904 and its Acme Brick is still beautiful in 2005.

Dennis Knautz rode with Buffett back to the airport that evening. "It was essentially a handshake deal," Knautz said. "He (Buffett) decides what a business was worth. And he liked the look of the management team. He told us, 'I bought you to run this business.'"[11]

Melton admitted to being impressed by the company's new owner. "I've been around a lot of bright people in my life," he said, "but I have never seen anyone who grasps the essence of a business the way Warren Buffett does. It doesn't take long for him to make a decision. He is really, really quick."[12]

Joining the Berkshire Hathaway Family

Warren Buffett left Fort Worth that June evening with the decision already made to purchase Justin Industries and its Acme Brick Company and Boot and Footwear subsidiaries. Buffett sent Bob Dinnen, his attorney, with an offer to buy Justin Industries for $22 a share, along with a contract. Dinnen told John Roach that Buffett wanted the contract signed as soon as possible. Roach told his staff to contact Omaha for due diligence, and he and Justin would sign the contract the following Monday or Tuesday.

"Due diligence involved a few questions about tax liabilities and insurance reserves," said Judy Hunter, who was then Justin Industries' corporate controller. "The contract was signed that Tuesday, a $600 million deal that was agreed to so quickly. The sale closed on August 1, 2000."[13]

Buffett met with the Justin Industries Board of Directors at the Fort Worth City Club the evening of August 1, and returned to Omaha the next day. Marc Hamburg, the chief financial officer of Berkshire Hathaway, met with the Justin Industries staff and explained that the holding company would disappear, and the boot company and Acme Brick Company would report to Berkshire Hathaway separately.

Harrold Melton, for one, was happy with the arrangement. "That took a lot of overhead out of our business," he said.[14] Hunter, who moved from the holding company to Acme Brick Company, worked closely for the next eighteen months with her counterparts in Omaha. "We split up the common accounting issues," she said, "and we separated employee benefits. We didn't change our reporting format. It was pretty simple. They only had fifteen or so people in their corporate office in Omaha. The transition was completed in December 2001."[15]

The Acme Brick Boys appear with two of the Fruit of the Loom mascots at the Berkshire Hathaway shareholders meeting in Omaha, Nebraska, in 2004.

Warren Buffet considered Acme Brick one of his better investments.

Melton told employees that the acquisition by Berkshire Hathaway would be good for Acme Brick Company. "The acquisition will be a very beneficial thing for Acme's homebuilder customers," Melton said. "All the things that Mr. Buffett and Berkshire Hathaway believe in—continuity, sound conservative business practices, and growth with stability—are excellent fits with Acme Brick Company's century-old philosophy. Our new ownership will enable Acme Building Brands to continue making the necessary investments in manufacturing and distribution to stay abreast of our customers' growing needs. The acquisition will provide ever improving products and services, and more selections for Acme's customers."[16]

Continuing Expansion

During the negotiations with Buffett and the transition to Berkshire Hathaway ownership, John Justin's health had deteriorated. Justin died in Fort Worth on Monday, February 26, 2001.[17] He was sorely missed by the Acme Brick Company community, but his death illustrated the wisdom he had shown in 1999 and 2000 to create an orderly transition for Justin Industries out of Justin family control.

Acme Brick Company, meanwhile, continued its strategy of acquiring brick plants and distribution facilities in the South Central United States. In July 2001, Acme Building Brands acquired the Holly Springs, Mississippi, Brick Plant from Hanson Brick America, a division of Hanson Building Materials America, Inc. The plant in Holly Springs was located in Northern Mississippi, some fifty miles southeast of Memphis, Tennessee.[18] The acquisition was in line with the company's strategy of acquiring plants capable of serving customers in metropolitan Memphis, and built on the recent purchase of Wheeler Brick Company in Jonesboro, Arkansas.

Harrold Melton noted that "over the last four years, Acme sales into the Memphis market have nearly tripled. Our purchase of this facility will provide an additional source of brick for our Memphis customers. . . . Acquiring this plant adds about 3 percent to our annual production capacity, and its location will allow us to improve our product offering and service level to our customers in support of our growing presence in the Memphis area as well as in Northern Mississippi."[19]

The Holly Springs acquisition came on the heels of Acme Brick Company's May 2001 purchase of Laufen International, Inc.'s tile distribution center located in Tulsa, Oklahoma. Laufen International said it planned to concentrate on the manufacture of ceramic tile at its Oklahoma plant. Acme Brick Company and American Tile Company had been Laufen International's

This 2004 calendar photo pairs Acme Brick with Justin Boots.

largest customer for a number of years. Adding the Tulsa distribution center would give American Tile a stronger presence in Oklahoma.[20]

Acme Brick Company went further afield in late 2001 when it acquired the Denver Brick Company in the Denver suburb of Castle Rock, Colorado. The tunnel kiln plant produced about 50 million brick per year, and was noted for its diverse product line and quality customer service through its nationwide distributor network.

Harrold Melton called the purchase "an exciting opportunity to expand into a completely new market for Acme Brick. Acquiring this plant adds about 5 percent to our annual production capacity."[21] Melton added that the acquisition was in line with Berkshire Hathaway's expansion policies. "Warren Buffett has enthusiastically supported and encouraged our strategy of production capacity that enables us to more adequately serve our customers," Melton told employees.[22]

Twenty-First Century Technology

Berkshire Hathaway expected that its companies stay technologically in step with the latest computer systems, and by the time Acme Brick Company joined the Warren Buttett family of companies, its BRIX system was more than a

Acme brick at the jobsite 2003.

quarter-century old. BRIX did pass the Y2K test, when many information technology departments were concerned about the ability of computer systems to transfer data from the twentieth century to the twenty-first century. But the Unisys-based BRIX system was out of date and needed to be replaced.

In July 2001, Acme Brick Company's management team made the decision to install a new computer system. Dubbed the Enterprise Resource Planning (ERP) project, the new system was brought to life when Acme Brick Company hired Rush Weston as its new technology director.[23] Weston, who had received his computer science degree from Southern Methodist University in 1981, had worked information technology jobs in the Metroplex since that time. He sold his IT business in Dallas in 1996 and joined Acme Brick Company.[24]

"In 2001," he said, "we had an aging mainframe. The technology was outdated. There were still good functions to BRIX, but the general ledger and order entry were on separate platforms."[25]

Weston pulled together a task force of fifty-five employees from around the Acme Brick Company system, and they spent 2001 narrowing the software search to three companies: Oracle, Baan, and J. D. Edwards. "Those fifty-five people voted for J. D. Edwards," Weston said. "IT voted for Oracle."[26]

Acme Brick Company finalized a contract with J. D. Edwards in the spring of 2002, and Weston implemented a seven-phase approach to making the new ERP system work. He picked twelve people as trainers, and they underwent six months of learning, tests, and conference room pilot programs. Over a three-year period, the trainers trained others on the intricacies of the ERP system. Phase I involved general ledger and accounts payable, and was completed in late 2002. Phase II involved

Acme urged prospective homebuyers to look for the Acme logo as a sign of quality in 2001.

customer and accounts receivable, Phase III got plant production on line, and Phase IV involved adding order entry, "all the way from order entry to collecting the cash."[27]

Phases V and VI put all the plant equipment maintenance records on line, and added American Tile Supply and its point of sale system to ERP. "That was a lot of bucket and trowel business," Weston said. The final Phase VII process converted the payroll and human resources system to ERP. The entire system went live in late 2003 and early 2004. J. D. Edwards was purchased by Oracle several years later, but Weston said "Oracle has done a good job of supporting J. D. Edwards projects."[28]

A New Team

Acme Brick Company ended 2004 with a strong performance. The 97 million brick equivalent shipped in December 2004 represented the highest brick volume ever for a December and a 4 percent gain over December 2003. The positive impact of record brick shipments and net sales in 2004 was a reflection of housing starts for the seven-state primary market that were higher than initial expectations. Brick margins for the year, however, were lower by 3.6 percent, due mostly to higher natural gas and diesel costs. In 2004, natural gas still comprised approximately 20 percent of the company's brick manufacturing costs. Looking forward into 2005, Acme Brick Company expected a slight drop in housing starts that would be offset by broader price increases.[29]

What would change for Acme Brick Company in 2005 was the company's leadership. In the spring of 2005, Harrold Melton concluded a forty-year career in the brick industry when he announced his retirement concurrent to being honored with the Brick Industry Association's 2005 Outstanding Achievement Award.[30]

Succeeding Melton as president and CEO in 2005 was Dennis D. Knautz, a twenty-three-year veteran of Acme Brick Company. Knautz, a Chicago-area native, had joined Acme Brick Company in 1982 as controller and was on Melton's executive management team as the company's Vice President of Finance. During his career, he had helped implement the company-wide BRIX computer system. Knautz had also been closely involved in developing many of Acme Brick's financial and administrative systems during the restructuring of Justin Industries and the later acquisition of the company by Berkshire Hathaway.[31]

In his inaugural message to the company and its workforce, Knautz noted that 2005 would go down as a year of management change. Retiring along with Melton was Robert L. "Bob" Stover, the company's Vice President of Sales. Stover capped a forty-one-year career with Acme Brick Company, having started with the firm in 1964 as an office manager at the company's research laboratory in Denton, Texas.[32]

Joining Knautz's executive management team were Stan McCarthy and Bill Lemond. McCarthy, a nineteen-year veteran, was named Vice President of Sales with responsibility for the Texas–New Mexico region.[33] Lemond, whose career with Acme Brick Company stretched back twenty-six years, was also named vice president of sales with responsibility for all areas outside Texas and New Mexico.[34]

In his first message to employees, Knautz said economic forecasts for the future were bright. "Economists who were cautious about the last half of this year now believe that construction activity will continue at a strong level," Knautz told employees in July 2005.[35]

And the economists were right, at least for the short term. Acme Brick Company would enjoy the best year in its long history in 2006. But the bullish run of the late 1990s and early twenty-first century would come to a grinding halt in 2008.

In 2005, Dennis Knautz appeared on the television show *Your New House* with Michael Holigan.

CHAPTER 10
NEW LEADERSHIP
2006 TO 2010

An Acme Brick truck sign in 2007 urges customers to go to brick.com.

Dennis Knautz presided over Acme Brick Company's 116th birthday on April 17, 2007. "Baby Clay," the world's largest brick, was born on July 4, 2007. During that summer, Baby Clay traveled to every one of Acme Brick Company's multi-state locations as part of the anniversary celebration. Business was strong in 2007. By year-end 2006, Acme Brick Company had set sales records for fifteen years in a row, since 1992. The company was in the process of converting the Elgin Handmades Plant to stiff mud extrusion, and was a leader in twenty-first century brickmaking. Acme Brick expanded into Minnesota in early 2008 with the acquisition of

Bricks from the Walter Bennett Brick Collection.

The end of an era—Acme Brick's Headquarters from 1952 to 2007.

Baby Clay in 2007 with its makers.

Ochs Brick Plant in Springfield, McFarlane Stone in Bloomington, and the Ochs Sales Office in Edina.

But the start of the second half of the first decade of the twenty-first century masked a major problem with the U.S. economy. The roots of the 2008–2009 recession were contained in subprime mortgage standards and escalating energy prices that pushed the United States into the worst economic crisis since the Great Depression. The ensuing housing collapse forced Acme Brick Company to reduce production at almost all of its

The Dallas/Fort Worth Sales Office in 2006.

plants, as well as the temporary closure of the Weir, Bridgeport, San Felipe, and Ouachita Plants in late 2007; the Holly Springs, Kanopolis, and Old Bennett Plants in 2008; and the Ochs, Perla Westgate, Eureka, Bennett, McQueeney, Garrison, Texas Clay "A," Tulsa, and Denver Plants in 2009.

But a management lesson passed down for generations paid dividends down the road. Acme Brick Company did not shut down a single sales office during the Great Recession. The company also used the downtime during the recession to refit and rehabilitate some of its older plants, including the rebuilding of a kiln at the San Felipe Plant and the installation of a monorail at the Ouachita Plant. As a result of solid management and committed associates, Acme Brick Company became the largest brick manufacturer, by volume, in the United States in 2008, a position it has maintained since. Still, housing starts hit a sixty-five-year low in 2009, and Acme Brick Company responded by running many of its plants only sparingly during 2009 and 2010. Because of the unprecedented economic conditions, Acme Brick made the reluctant decision to permanently close the Weir, Kansas Plant in 2010, the last operating brick plant that was part of the United Brick Division acquisition from 1963.

Shortly before the full brunt of the Great Recession hit Texas and the Southwest, Acme Brick Company relocated its

A NEW GENERAL OFFICE ON THE TRINITY RIVER

By 2006, Acme Brick's corporate office was bursting at the seams and spread throughout multiple buildings along West Seventh Street in Fort Worth. On October 6, the 154th birthday of founder George Bennett, President and CEO Dennis Knautz climbed aboard a New Holland backhoe/loader and scooped up the ceremonial first bucket of dirt to break ground for a new Acme Brick general office.[1]

The site for the new campus was a wooded plot at 3101 Bryant Irvin Road (which is now 3024 Acme Brick Plaza) on the bank of the Trinity River just southwest of downtown Fort Worth. The new general office would serve two main purposes: it would provide for current as well as future office and administrative needs, and it would serve as a showcase for the company's products. Gideon Toal Architects and Masonry Contractor Dee Brown Inc. were given the charge of incorporating brick material types from all of the company's twenty-one brick plants, as well as materials from Acme Brick's sister companies, including concrete block (CMU) from Featherlite Building Products, limestone from Texas Quarries, site unit pavers from Pacific Clay, and a special structural glass flooring system from IBP.[2]

Since it was a showcase for masonry, the new general office utilized many types of special coursing or patterning. Special attention was given to the necessity of laying masonry units to tight tolerances because of the building's signature representation of the nation's largest brick supplier. All told, the building contained forty-four thousand square feet of interior and exterior brick veneer, thirty-seven thousand square feet of CMU, eighty-eight hundred square feet of native Texas limestone in cut-to-size patterns, three hundred square feet of specialty glass flooring, thirty-three thousand square feet of site unit pavers, and multiple examples of artist-carved brick feature panels.[3]

Stone and masonry work was completed in just under a year, and the new Acme Brick general office opened in late 2007. In the summer of 2014, a reporter interviewed former Chairman Ed Stout in the building's top-floor boardroom. To the southwest, a frontal system featuring the roll clouds synonymous with a severe weather outbreak was visible and the reporter glanced back several times through the room's floor-to-ceiling windows.

Stout noticed the reporter's discomfort. "Son," he said, "you don't have to worry. This is an Acme Brick building."[4]

Acme Brick's Fort Worth Headquarters in 2004, fondly known to employees as the building with no windows.

headquarters from downtown Fort Worth to a new building on the banks of the Trinity River in the southwestern quadrant of the city; the company incorporated brick, block, stone, IBP Glass Block Grids, and tile from all Acme Brick Company facilities in the new building. The relocation was a visible reminder to the community that Acme Brick would be there for them, through good times and bad.

"A Teamwork Deal"

Baby Clay was the brainchild of Ron Taylor, who handled Acme Brick's public relations account. At Ron's direction, Seidel approached Harland Dixson, manager of the Denton Plant, sometime in early 2007 about the plant's ability to make the world's largest brick to mark Acme Brick Company's 116th anniversary.

"I said, yeah, we can do that," Dixson recalled. "I got Mack Wilcox and several others from the plant management team together, and we began planning how we would do it."[1] Forming and firing the 118-inch brick was a trial and error process. "We made four of them before we got it right," Dixson said. "The fifth one made it happen. It was July 4, 2007."[2]

Dennis Knautz cuts the mammoth 115th Berk-Day cake in 2006; the cake contains logos of all the companies in which Berkshire Hathaway has a major investment.

Seidel and the executive team scheduled Baby Clay for a tour of all of Acme Brick's facilities. "We got a lot of publicity," Dixson recalled. "We actually made it in the 2009 *Guinness Book of World Records*. We took it to the Berkshire Hathaway Annual Meeting in Omaha. It was definitely a teamwork deal. We did make it happen."[3]

The Denton Plant had been making it happen for years. In the twenty-first century, the facility had provided close to seven hundred thousand brick for the Ballpark at Arlington, 1.2 million brick for the Brooks Air Force Base Medical Center at San Antonio, Texas, and brick for the Tarrant County Jail and Courthouse in downtown Fort Worth. For Dixson and his Denton team, Baby Clay was just another challenge.

For Dennis Knautz and his executive team in Fort Worth, the "can do" attitude of employees like Dixson was one of the key reasons Acme Brick had enjoyed the success it had. Knautz, who had succeeded Harrold Melton in early 2005 at the helm of Acme Brick, had experienced fifteen years of record growth, one year after another. "In early 2006," he said, "things are still going great. We were primarily looking for ways to maximize earnings."[4]

In April 2006, Knautz cut a giant cake for a Berkshire Hathaway-themed birthday. The cake, which celebrated the company's "115th Berk-Day" at the annual service awards luncheon, was a giant-sized replica of a commemorative towel distributed to all company employees. Logos on the cake's frosting represented companies like Coca-Cola and Wal-

Mart, in which Berkshire Hathaway held a major common stock ownership position.[5] Since 1991, Acme Brick has a tradition of distributing presents to its associates on the company's birthday.

Knautz and his executive team could be forgiven for believing that the trajectory of supplying brick for new residential housing would continue ever upward. "We had enjoyed nineteen years of better, better, better," Knautz said. "We had discussions around this board table that the economic cycles of the past were over."[6]

They weren't. And the resulting recession shook the American economy to its very foundation. There were times in the fall of 2008 when policymakers in Washington, D.C., and on Wall Street were bracing themselves for another Great Depression.

"Orders Kept Falling the Rest of the Year"

Residential housing was ground zero of what became known as the Great Recession, and companies that built houses or supplied materials for the building of houses were the first to feel the effects of an economic upheaval unprecedented since the October 1929 collapse of the Wall Street stock market. For years, America's banks and lending institutions had played fast and loose with lending standards for residential homeowners. Encouraged by politicians who believed that everyone had the right to be a homeowner, lending institutions, including the federally backed chartered lenders Federal National Mortgage Agency (Fannie Mae) and the Federal Home Loan Mortgage Corporation (Freddie Mac), created a subprime mortgage catastrophe that would bring the American economy to its knees. By 2006, trillions of dollars in mortgages were in the process of being foreclosed; millions of homeowners owed more on their mortgages than their houses were actually worth.

"We saw the crazy mortgages and lending happening," Knautz said, but nobody wanted to believe that subprime mortgages had the capability of torpedoing the American economy. For Acme Brick, July 2006 marked the beginning of the Great Recession. "We had been booking 100 million brick a month through 2006," Knautz said. "We booked 80 million brick in July 2006, and it kept falling every month for the rest of the year."[7]

The rest of the economy began unraveling in 2007 and accelerated into 2008. Old-line investment-banking houses like Bear Stearns and Lehman Brothers were victims of the liquidity crisis. By September 2008, the federal government had stepped in with a multitrillion rescue for the battered national economy.

Housing, Acme Brick Company's bread and butter, took a crippling hit. Between 2006 and 2010, housing starts in the

Acme Brick's Burk Burnett Building was built in 1914 and has stood the test of time.

ACME BRICK COMPANY

ENVIRONMENTAL/SUSTAINABILITY STATEMENT

September 28, 2007

Acme Brick Company is committed to conducting business in an environmentally responsible manner. By proactively developing policies and procedures that exceed minimum standards, by utilizing our environmental management system, and through employee awareness, we will strive for compliance with all applicable environmental rules and regulations. Acme will maintain our sustainable practices through business planning and continuous improvement of manufactured products, services, and operations.

Acme Brick Company will establish goals and objectives, in a responsible manner, to employ building management, mining, manufacturing, and delivery techniques that will:

- Minimize the impact on our natural resources,
- Optimize consumption of energy and raw material supplies, and
- Eliminate and recycle waste,

while, at the same time, providing long life-cycle products of enduring quality and value for our customers.

The Senior Management of Acme Brick Company endorses this statement:

Dennis Knautz
President and Chief Executive Officer

Ed Watson
Senior Vice President of Production

Judy Hunter
Chief Financial Officer

Bill Seidel
Senior Vice President of Marketing

Bill Lemond
Senior Vice President of Sales

Stan McCarthy
Senior Vice President of Sales

Acme Brick pledged to protect the environment in this 2007 Environmental Sustainability Statement.

Dennis Knautz lighting up for Acme Brick's 118th birthday in 2009.

Memphis market, for example, dropped by more than 90 percent. And Acme Brick felt fortunate that it wasn't serving markets like California, Arizona, Nevada, and South Florida that were absolutely devastated by the liquidity crisis. "We didn't have a lot of mortgage flipping in Texas like they did elsewhere," Knautz said. "We're blessed that the state has a good business climate."[8]

The depression in housing rippled right back to the national brick industry, however. The industry shipped 9.5 billion brick in 2006; by 2010, the industry struggled to ship 2.5 billion brick. "It's a business with high capital and fixed costs," Knautz explained. "When business starts declining like it did, people cut price to maintain volume."

Knautz told employees in the summer of 2007 that "we have arrived at the halfway point of 2007, and it appears that the second half of this year will be as challenging and difficult as we have seen in the last twenty years."[9] Knautz went on to explain that "our business is more closely aligned with residential activity than any other segment of the

construction industry. Through the first five months of this year, housing starts in our sales territory have fallen by a stunning 21 percent below the same period last year."[10]

Housing starts and brick sales continued to fall. By December 2007, brick shipments were down 28 percent for the month, and 29 percent year-to-date. December marked the twenty-first consecutive month in decline in year-over-year comparisons; the month represented Acme Brick's lowest volume month in a decade.[11] Brick wasn't the only product line to suffer during the Great Recession. In December 2007, the company wrote off $2.8 million in goodwill on its American Tile investment; as a result of the terrible economic conditions, the company's 2007 total net sales were off nearly 20 percent, a drop of $100 million from 2006.[12]

Joan Wylie, the first woman to win the President's Award, at the Managers' Meeting at Texas Motor Speedway in 2006.

Business in 2008 was no better. By December, average brick shipments had dipped to 2,064 MBE per day, the lowest rate since January 1992 and less than half what they were in late 2005. And business activity actually seemed to be slowing. The company reported that bookings of new orders had slipped below 39,000 MBE for the second consecutive month, "an indication that shipping comparisons to prior year levels will continue to disappoint for the first quarter of 2009."[13]

Margins on brick sales continued to drop, down nearly 14 percent in 2008. The impact of lower production rates and higher natural gas costs promised to suppress margins for several years to come. There was little the company could do but cut back to ride out the storm. Between 2006 and 2008, Acme Brick laid off nearly half its thirty-one hundred associates. The company shut down half of its brick plants. "We tried to match the production rate with our sales," Knautz said.

The efforts were to little avail. Results in 2009 were a disaster. The company put a brave face on things, calling it "a disappointing year." Sharply lower sales volume and selling price in December 2009 reduced gross profit by 27 percent and led to the worst monthly operating result since January 2009 and the first known operating loss since the Great Depression. For the entire year, the company lost more than $10 million.[14]

"There was really no record we could find of Acme Brick ever losing money," Knautz said about the 2009 results. "And then we lost money every year from 2009 to 2013, for five years in a row."[15] The Great Recession was perhaps one of the

more humbling periods in Acme Brick's 125-year history, but the company understood that the cycles driving an inherently cyclical business would bring back good times again.

Embracing Opportunity

From its earliest days, Acme Brick and its leadership had always realized that difficult times were uniquely positioned for taking advantage of opportunities. A good example was the work Acme Brick did to upgrade the Elgin New Plant in 2007. While the liquidity crisis was depressing housing starts and brick sales, Acme Brick crews completed a major renovation of the plant, designed to increase production rates while delivering greater efficiency to brickmaking at Elgin. Crews removed the existing Dutch brick molding machinery and replaced it with a high-capacity J. C. Steele 90 Extruder.[16] Although the New Elgin Plant would not return to full capacity until after 2012, the upgrades and modifications would ensure that it would be a state-of-the-art facility capable of giving Acme Brick a competitive edge.

Another example of the company's ability to see advantages where others saw only crises involved the spring 2008 decision

Acme Brick's General Production Manager Jerry Hodge with his President's Award in 2006.

Russ Weston holding the President's Award in 2007 on behalf of his IT team.

to purchase Ochs Brick and Stone and McFarlane Stone in far-off Minnesota. The privately held Minnesota company had run head-on into the brick wall of plunging housing starts and had idled its kilns at Springfield, on the Minnesota prairie about an hour's drive southwest of the Twin Cities. The company had lost a bid to provide brick for the new University of Minnesota football stadium, and the owners reluctantly had decided to get out of the business. In December 2007, Dennis Knautz picked up the phone and asked owners Matt and Peggy Van Hoomissen if they would be interested in Acme Brick acquiring them. They were, and the deal was announced in February 2008.

Van Hoomissen told a reporter from the Twin Cities that he had no hesitation in merging with Acme Brick because "they have a wonderful, wonderful reputation in the business."[17] The acquisition was an excellent fit for Acme Brick's future

growth. The company's farthest northern sales territories were in Kansas and Missouri, and the Twin Cities were one of the most dynamic metropolitan markets north of Kansas City.

Still, the culture shock of closing an acquisition on the rural Minnesota prairies in February is part of the Acme Brick legend. Joan Wylie, considered by many to be the finest President's Award winner, was on the team that integrated Ochs into the Acme Brick system and recalled the trip. "We flew into Mankato, Minnesota, in February," she said. "I never warmed up. Springfield had one motel, a Microtel."[18]

The Great Recession years tested Acme Brick like no other event in the company's long history. But the company emerged from the fires of the worst economic upheaval since the Great Depression tempered and ready for the challenges of the second decade of the twenty-first century.

CHAPTER 11
RECOVERING AGAIN

2011 TO 2015

Aerial view of the Birmingham Plant that was part of the Jenkins Brick acquisition.

A stamped Acme Brick from 2011.

The recovery from the Great Recession was a long and difficult struggle. Acme Brick Company continued to contend with a weak regional and national economy through 2011, even while the company worked to minimize collection losses caused by the collapse of the housing sector to near zero by mid-2011. The recovery in the housing market picked up steam in 2012, particularly in Texas and the Southwest. Acme Brick's manufactured brick backlog increased 34 percent between mid-2011 and mid-2012. The company experienced sharp increases in stone sales in 2012, and Acme Brick responded by continuing to increase sales and production rates in 2013. It wasn't until 2014, however, that Acme Brick broke its five-year streak of annual losses, the first in the company's long history.

The Great Recession was global in scope, and brick and stone manufacturers from around the world felt the effects of the slowdown. The company's performance against Boral and General Shale, its two largest competitors, was strong in the wake of the Great

Dennis Knautz guided Acme Brick through the worst recession since the 1930s.

Recession; Acme Brick Company continued to maintain a dominant and strengthening position into 2012, especially in light of the consolidation in the brick industry in North America during the twenty-first century.

One way Acme Brick exercised its influence was through the company's 2010 strategic initiative that created shared values, cultural beliefs and goals for Acme Brick Company's workforce. Acme took a growing leadership role in the Brick Industry Association (BIA) on a host of issues important to the industry. Dennis Knautz served two terms as president of BIA and helped defeat the Kyle, Texas lawsuit that threatened to hamper the industry.

Jenkins Brick

The January 2011 acquisition of Jenkins Brick Company from the Mike Jenkins family, with three plants in Alabama and sixteen sales offices across five Southeastern states, was a signal to the industry that Acme Brick had no intention of lying low during the continuing difficult times kicked off by the Great Recession.

Acme Brick had become better acquainted with Jenkins Brick following its purchase of Edmonds Materials in 2005, and Dennis Knautz and his management team knew they would like

Dennis Knoutz sparks an Acme birthday cake in 2013.

to have the brand identification of Jenkins Brick in the Mid-South when the recovery from the Great Recession was finally in full swing. "Jenkins had been identified as an attractive partner for us early on," said Bill Lemond, Acme Brick Vice President since 2005. "We were on the Gulf Coast of Mississippi, and Jenkins had a major presence in Middle Mississippi and Northern Mississippi. Jenkins was even our distributor in some markets."[1]

Lemond had long been familiar with Jenkins Brick, and he noted "the Edmonds acquisition was a huge factor in our ability to later acquire Jenkins Brick."[2] Lemond and his wife had a daughter in Huntsville, Alabama, at the time, and when they would visit her, Lemond would often drop by the local Jenkins office in Huntsville.

By 2010, the Alabama company had run into debt problems traced to the Great Recession, and Mike Jenkins was actively seeking a buyer. Jenkins, who headed the family-owned company wasn't sure he wanted to sell to Acme Brick, but during 2010, Jenkins Brick management essentially convinced him it was the smartest thing he could do. When the Brick Forum met in North Carolina in January 2011, Dennis Knautz and Mike Jenkins met the weekend prior to the Monday morning start of the Forum. Knautz conveyed an offer to Jenkins, but the Acme Brick team left North Carolina midweek with no word from Jenkins about their offer.

The Friday afternoon following the Forum, Knautz and the leadership team received word that Mike Jenkins agreed to the Acme Brick offer. A deal was struck and announced on February 1, 2011.[3] The highlight of the year, Dennis Knautz pointed out, "was the purchase of Jenkins Brick Company and adding more than three hundred wonderful associates to our payroll. What a talented group of people who share the same enthusiasms and passions for our business as most of us do. They have been quite helpful and very patient as we have taken steps to integrate them into our company."[4]

Lemond viewed the acquisition as a no-brainer. "The Jenkins business model paralleled the Acme Brick business model," he said. "Jenkins did sell brick from other manufacturers and actually had a higher percentage on nonbrick sales than Acme. They were a market leader. There was just a lot of fit between their culture and ours. It gave us a common definition."[5]

Knautz and his leadership team spent much of 2011 integrating Jenkins Brick into the Acme Brick structure. Stone and granite operations were moved to the Coosada Plant north of Montgomery, Alabama, and the Montgomery sales yard began hosting a regional sales office.[6] During November 2011,

THE LIFE AND CAREER OF DENNIS KNAUTZ

Dennis Knautz had never stepped foot in the state of Texas prior to enrolling at Texas Christian University (TCU) in the fall of 1971. He had grown up in the North Shore suburbs of Chicago and played hockey for Deerfield High School, where he gradated in 1971. Knautz hoped to play hockey in college and had set his sights on enrolling at the University of Denver, which played in the then dominant Western Collegiate Hockey Association (WCHA). But when Knautz and his parents arrived for a visit at the UD campus, the school was closed for a Vietnam War sit-in. "Mom nixed UD," Knautz said.[1]

The 1970 and 1971 Cotton Bowl games in Dallas featured the University of Notre Dame and the University of Texas in battles for the national collegiate football championship, and Knautz, a Notre Dame fan growing up, eagerly followed both games. He remembers being particularly impressed by the UT cheerleaders at halftime of the football games. "Hey," he said, "we were all eighteen once."[2]

The University of Texas seemed a little bit overwhelming, but in researching other Texas schools, Knautz and his parents found themselves favorably impressed with Texas Christian. "TCU was not an unknown name on the North Shore," he said. "Plus, it had the advantage of being quite a bit smaller than UT."[3] Knautz did his undergraduate and graduate work at TCU in mathematics and earned an MBA in 1976. He was working part time at City Transportation Service while pursuing the MBA and went full time with the municipal transportation agency after earning his MBA.

Knautz worked for Bill Lemond at City Transit in 1977 and 1978. Lemond moved to Acme Brick that year, and Knautz pursued his CPA at the University of Texas–Arlington while continuing to work for City Transportation. In 1982, he received a call from Acme Brick. Bill Lemond was working as a special assistant to Ed Stout at the time, and he told Knautz the company needed to hire a financial officer. Knautz joined Acme Brick as controller in August 1982.

"I saw in the early 1980s that City Transit was run through the public sector," Knautz said. "There was no profit incentive. City Transit was a service business."[4] Knautz saw an opportunity with Acme Brick to grow: from the public to the private sector, and from the service industry to manufacturing. He worked his way up through the 1990s to vice president of finance and then to chief financial officer by the time Ed Stout announced his retirement in 1999.

With the succession of Harrold Melton to president and the acquisition of Acme Brick by Warren Buffett's Berkshire Hathaway conglomerate, Knautz's financial responsibilities continued to increase. In 2004, Harrold Melton told Knautz he intended to retire the following April, and he had recommended Knautz succeed him as president. Knautz was named as executive vice president and chief operating officer (COO) to help smooth out the transition.

During Knautz's tenure as president and CEO, Acme Brick, like the rest of the industry, struggled with the housing collapse and the Great Recession. Knautz and his leadership team skillfully maneuvered Acme Brick through a lengthy period of cost cutting, plant upgrades, and acquisitions.

Knautz also established a position of leadership in the regional Southwest Brick Council and the national Brick Industry Association, serving two terms as BIA chairman. During his tenure with BIA, the association encouraged municipalities to adopt masonry ordinances that would require the use of brick in residential construction. When the city of Kyle, Texas, became the target of a lawsuit filed by the National Association of Homebuilders for its development ordinance requiring the use of brick in construction, Knautz helped convince BIA that the Kyle lawsuit was a line in the sand.

In March 2009, a Federal District Court rejected the legal challenge. In November 2010, the U.S. Fifth Circuit Court of Appeals rejected the appeal filed by the plaintiffs.

"We now have some two hundred municipalities in Texas that have masonry regulations similar to those of Kyle," Knautz said.[5]

a group of Jenkins associates traveled to Fort Worth to visit the Acme Brick general offices; while there, most trained on the company's J. D. Edwards ERP system. By early 2012, most of the Jenkins offices were on-line with the Acme Brick J. D. Edwards payroll system.[7]

Jenkins associates also began familiarizing themselves with "The Acme Way," a mission and vision statement adopted in 2010 that incorporated key beliefs and key results. In his column in *The Brick Press*, Dennis Knautz noted the new Mission Statement called for Acme Brick Associates to "continually

improve the value of our company. Most of our efforts—and those highlighted in these pages—support one or more of the guiding principles that define how we are to grow our company's value over time."[8] Knautz specifically pointed to "the Jenkins associates' efforts to help generate more than $100,000 for the American Red Cross" as a demonstration of the company's serving as a positive influence in the communities in which it operates.[9]

Jay Isenhour (left) receives the 2013 Plant Manager of the Year Award from Acme's Senior Vice President of Production Ed Watson.

A Slow Recovery

Since the recession began affecting company operations in 2006, revenues had plummeted. Acme Brick had reported revenues of just over $550 million in 2006. In five years, revenues had plunged $200 million, to $300 million at the end of 2010.[10] "It was 5-1/2 years ago when we saw a sharp decline in orders that in hindsight signaled the inception of the longest, deepest downturn in our industry's history," the company reported in December 2011. "Net sales in 2011 for our core Acme operations were half what they were in 2006, and the $90 million operating profit we recorded that year contrasts sharply with the $20 million loss for the year just ended."[11]

Despite the difficult recovery, Acme Brick could take some solace in the fact that the company benchmarked well against its principal competitors. The Jenkins Brick acquisition was symbolic of the consolidation that had been underway in the North American brick industry since the late 1990s and that was accelerating in the wake of the Great Recession. Acme Brick, Boral, and General Shale had emerged as the continent's three largest brick manufacturers.

In December 2011, the Acme Brick leadership team compared the company's consolidated sales to those of Boral and General Shale, from the fourth quarter of 2003 through the end of 2011. With sales of nearly $350 million in 2011, Acme Brick was $150 million ahead of second place General Shale and $200 million ahead of Boral. "While all three companies have recorded

Jose Reya carving limestone at the Texas Quarries Plant.

Acme associate Tanilo Gonzalez.

Grand Opening of the New Orleans sales office in 2014.

significant declines in revenue since 2006," Acme Brick reported, "it is evident that Acme still has a dominant and strengthening position, particularly with the addition of Jenkins in 2011."[12]

The company's performance in 2012 wasn't much better. The year ended with an $18 million loss—just marginally better than the loss reported in 2011—and the 740 million brick delivered in 2012 was the lowest annual total in a quarter-century.[13] Recovery quickened in 2013. The company was able to increase sales by $35 million and cut its operating losses by nearly $12 million compared to 2012. At midyear, there was hope that the company might break even or show a small profit for the year. But a combination of slightly higher mortgage interest rates, economic uncertainty, and weather conditions resulted in less-than-hoped-for growth during the third and fourth quarters of the year. It would not be until 2014 that Acme Brick broke its five-year streak of red ink.[14]

One casualty of the agonizingly slow recovery between 2011 and 2014 was the company's foray into upscale tile and home furnishings stores. In the spring of 2011, Acme Brick held grand openings for three Patina Floor Design stores in the Dallas–Fort Worth Metroplex.[15] The stores, located in the Chapel Hill neighborhood of Fort Worth, on Knox Street in Dallas, and at Southlake, Texas, were a retail concept designed by Gensler Architects and employed degreed designers. Acme Brick Company had been searching for a way to jumpstart American Tile since they assumed responsibility for the subsidiary in 2004.

"American Tile never really gained traction in retail," Acme Brick Company Vice President Stan McCarthy said.

Dennis Knautz standing in front of the brick sculpture that adorns the reception area in the Acme Brick corporate office.

Associates packaging brick at the Denton Plant.

"We started consolidating stores in 2008 and shut down locations in Dallas, Houston, and elsewhere. We actually brought consultants in to right-size American Tile. We got inventories under control, but we were still not hitting sales numbers."[16]

In 2010, in the midst of the Great Recession, Acme Brick took a risk by starting up Patina. It was in character with the Acme Brick mission and vision statement. The company had always been willing during the tough times to expand in an attempt to grow out of recession.

"They were beautiful stores in very good locations," McCarthy said. "But they were high-cost stores, and we quickly found out how competitive the retail tile business was. We just didn't grow Patina fast enough."[17]

Another characteristic of the Acme Brick culture was the ability to admit something wasn't working and cut losses. In late 2013, Acme Brick announced it was taking a $3 million write-off and closing the Patina stores. Bob Hendon, a flooring veteran, was brought in to run American Tile, and he quickly

adopted a new strategic direction that would lead to significantly increasing American Tile's sales to Patina's former competitors.[18]

"Bob came in and realized we needed a two-step distribution model," McCarthy said. "We didn't want all our eggs in one basket. As a result, American Tile sales were up 30 percent in 2014."[19]

But there was also definite reason for optimism about the future by 2013. On February 5, the company hosted a community reception in honor of the first load of brick produced at the newly reopened Bennett Plant. Opened in 1996 and located on the site of Acme Brick's first brickmaking facility, dating to 1891, brickmaking came back to Bennett. Dennis Knautz also reported that the company was reopening a portion of its Texas Clay Plant located in Malakoff near Athens, Texas.

"It's very exciting to see this brick plant back in the business of making quality brick for our nation's homes," Knautz said. "Over the course of the past year, we have seen a rebirth of activity here in the Metroplex with construction now totaling 83 million square feet and forecasted to rise by double digits in 2013."[20]

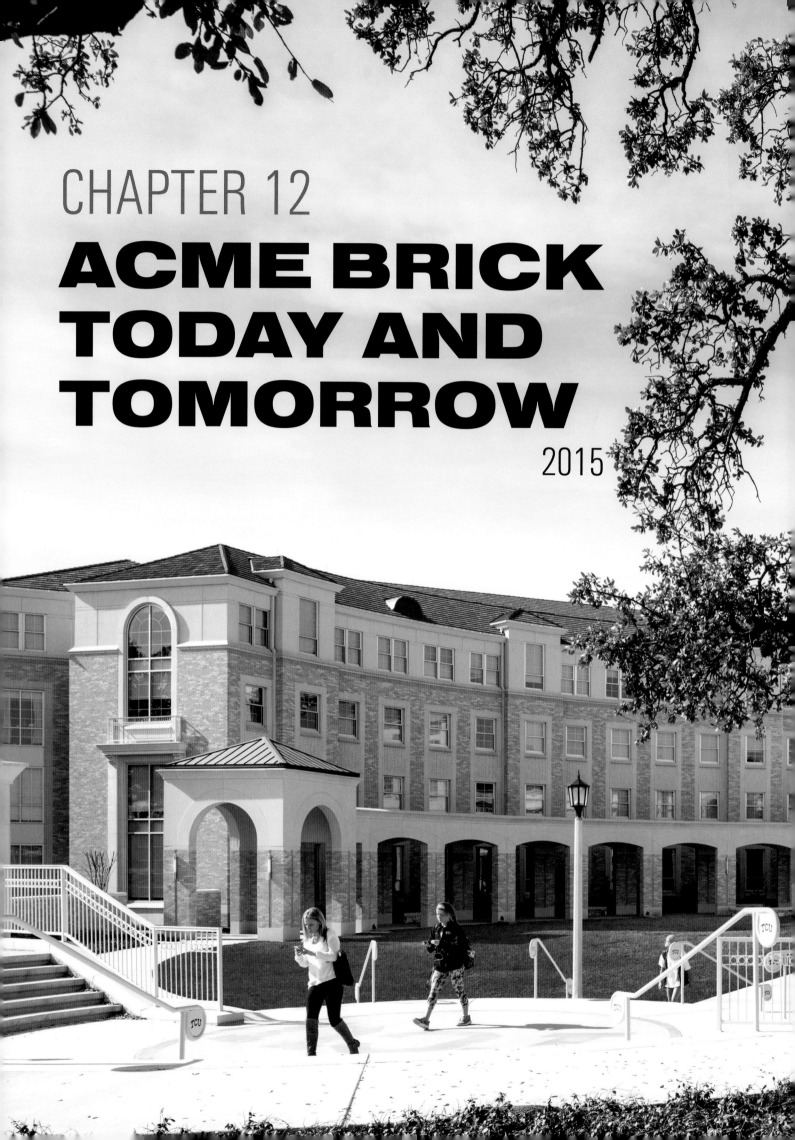

CHAPTER 12
ACME BRICK TODAY AND TOMORROW
2015

MARION HALL

CLARK

McLane Stadium on the Waco Campus.

Acme Brick Company today is a brickmaking colossus with plants and distribution facilities across Texas, the South, and Great Plains states. Acme Brick Company supplies a host of brands and product types to residential, commercial, and industrial customers around the country. Acme Brick can trace its success over the past century-and-a-quarter to the company's management and the company's associates, past and present; associates continue to be the engine that has driven Acme Brick Company's success for the past 125 years. The challenges faced by Acme Brick Company, its executives, and associates

These plaques list twenty-eight-years'-worth of outstanding Acme employees who were recognized with the President's Award.

Acme Perla Brick adorns the campus of TCU.

Associates at the Denton Plant (left to right): Reinaldo Roman, Thomas Rojas, Alexis Mendoza, Francisco Trevino, and Francisco Nicasio.

Acme has a bright future as part of Warren Buffett's Berkshire Hathaway. Buffett is shown here within the brick mural at Acme's Corporate Office.

today are really no more difficult than the challenges faced by executives and associates during the past 125 years of operation. Acme Brick Company's permanence and its innovation in basic brickmaking applications are hallmarks of the company's long history. Acme Brick's attention to cost efficiency in a competitive marketplace are everlasting strengths can be traced to that first brick plant in Bennett, Texas.

For Dennis Knautz, the Acme Brick president and CEO, Acme Brick is a different business to manage than it was when he first joined the company in 1982. The company now operates twenty-six brick plants, six block plants, and seventy sales offices across seventeen states stretching from Texas north to Minnesota and east to Tennessee and

Above: Cook Children's Hospital in Fort Worth.

Right: The interior walls of St. John's School in Houston, Texas, are crafted from Texas Quarries Stone.

Alabama. Acme Brick also sells to a nationwide network of independent distributors. "There was a lot more delegation when I first joined the company," he said. "We wanted to become a national brick company. That was part of the course we charted for the company. But to do that, you have to manage the business differently."[1]

Knautz, who was recently named "Top CEO of a Public Company for 2015" by *Fort Worth Business* magazine, has guided Acme Brick through a challenging decade that included the best of times and the worst of times.[2]

The worst of times had begun in the summer of 2006. Knautz and his leadership team watched brick orders fall by 20 percent in a single month. Instead of slashing the payroll and closing offices, Knautz took a more measured approach, viewing the downturn as an opportunity to prepare for the following spring. Surely, orders would pick up by then, he thought. "Spring came and it just got worse," said Knautz, who idled sixteen plants, including six in Texas. The company's workforce was cut as a result. "We had to get small. It was tough," Knautz said.[3]

Acme Brick President's Meeting on February 17, 2016

Front Row: Bob Hendon, Stan McCarthy, Judy Hunter, Elaine Suleski, Bill Lemond, Lisa Haile, Rusty Haile, Dennis Knautz, Ben Muro, Ed Watson, Nancy Menking, Marisela Taylor, and Rush Weston.

Second Row: Tracy Bruton, Mike Schrab, David McGrady, Brandon Hughes, Bill Daidone, Mike Anderson, Luke Odenthal, Garth Tayler, Joe Ward, Arthur Maina, Troy Russom, Ron Carbonaro, Jeff Joyce, Steve Weddle, Britt Stokes, Jesse Glaesman, Clark Burns, Jeremy Hargrave, Ron Benningfield, and Jeff Ringness.

Third Row: Trey Atwood, Matt Fels, Leon Hawk, Mark Burden, Brent Snyder, Harland Dixson, Marc McMillin, Kevin Story, Rodney Ebeling, Tom Brown, Terry Mackenzie, Norris Watson, Yulonda Charles, Bill Davis, Lisa Keye, Don Koesling, William Richardson, Mark Merchant, James Krueger, Les Seaton, Jay Cox, and David Michie.

Fourth Row: Paul Morgan, Michael Sutter, Lynn Burchfield, Bill Latham, Ladue Fossett, Kirk Martin, Bobby Harris, Tom Jeter, Brian Christenson, John Brewer, Bud Trussell, John Harp, John Fought, Ryan Hawkins, and Jason Winner.

Knautz and the Acme Brick leadership looked to lessons of the past to help guide them through the difficult economic conditions of the post-2006 period. Despite idling operations at several plants, no sales offices were shut down. "If you close a sales office, you're leaving that market. It's like pulling your hand out of a bucket of sand. It's harder to get back in," said Knautz.[4] "Not closing the sales offices was critical to maintaining that footprint from the sales side."[5] He credited Berkshire Hathaway's backing for his ability to downsize less than he otherwise might have.

Knautz noted that the experience of groping through the Great Recession without a defined roadmap helped convince Acme Brick leadership of the need to define cultural beliefs and key results. "We hadn't ever really articulated our culture," Knautz said. "It gave everybody in the company a common vocabulary. It was truly powerful."[6]

The company's cultural beliefs stress lifetime customers, doing right, taking ownership, building trust, embracing improvement, creating one team, and enhancing associates. That

Acme Brick comes in all size and shapes.

Estate Size Brick, shown here with the smaller Queen Size, added to Acme's shipments in 2016.

Acme's Technical Director Dr. Garth Tayler.

Acme CEOs from the past and the present (from left to right) Ed Stout, Dennis Knautz, and Harrold Melton.

in turn leads to "The Results Pyramid: Experiences, Beliefs, Actions, and Results." Associates from newest hires to oldest hands take the steps to accountability that leads to corporate success. They see it, own it, solve it, and do it.

The culture study revealed a close connectivity among the people, something that Knautz has frequently seen during his decade at the helm of Acme Brick. Knautz makes a point of spending as much time in the field as possible. "I travel a lot," said Knautz, who spent half his working days out of town during the fall of 2015 visiting Acme's seventy sales offices spread around fifteen states. "If I go to a market, it gives me a chance to understand what business conditions those markets are in. Keeping up is very important."[7] In any given year, Knautz tries to visit at least half the company's facilities. "I enjoy doing that," he said.[8]

Reasons for Optimism

After a stop-and-start recovery that has consumed much of the past decade, Acme Brick is finally seeing reasons to be optimistic about the future. A resurging housing industry is making business better for Knautz and Acme Brick these days.

"We're starting 2016 budget planning now and are looking at next year's demand," he said. He foresees greater demand for Acme products as builders construct new homes.

But even with the prospects for better days ahead, Knautz noted that navigating the shoals of a changing industry will require skill, sensitivity, and luck in the years to come. He pointed out that one hundred years ago there were more than two thousand brick manufacturers in the United States, most what the industry called "Mom and Pops." Today, there are fewer than sixty industrial brick manufacturers; the top five or six manufacturers, including Acme Brick, account for an estimated two-thirds of total industry capacity in 2015. And of those top five manufacturers, only Acme Brick remains American-owned.[9]

There are things about the industry that don't change, however, which ironically drive much of the change the industry is experiencing in the twenty-first century. "Brick is heavy," Knautz said. "It doesn't travel well. The natural delivery radius is about 250 miles around the brick manufacturing plant."[10]

Knautz pointed out another traditional reality that will continue to drive change in the industry. "The brick industry

Purchased products such as stone and iron doors will be a growing segment of future sales.

has a major barrier to entry," he said. "It requires a large amount of capital investment. Because of that, it's an industry that still has a potential for consolidation. The Mom and Pops have had some miserable years. The question is, are the bankers going to be willing to back the Mom and Pops financially? And that fact could introduce a new wave of consolidations."[11]

Despite the fact that Acme Brick is one of the largest brick manufacturers in the United States, Knautz doesn't consider the company a big business. "We have fewer than seventy sales offices," he said. "We are not a big business. We are a series of small businesses."[12]

That doesn't mean that Acme Brick isn't frequently treated like big business by government regulators. Acme Brick and the industry is currently wrestling with proposed air emission rules from the federal Environmental Protection Agency (EPA) designed to control greenhouse gas emissions.

"The EPA issued the rule in 2007," Knautz said, "but the Sierra Club went to court to vacate the rule because they felt it was not stringent enough. It's going to cost $1 to 1.5 million to install new scrubbers on every brick plant in the United States."[13]

Regardless of the challenges and opportunities that Acme Brick faces in the years to come, the company, its leadership and associates will face the future secure in the knowledge that every generation of associates in the company's 125-year history has surmounted challenges and taken advantage of opportunities on the way to making Acme Brick one of the premier brick manufacturers in the world.

George Bennett, no doubt, would understand.

NOTES

Chapter 1

1. Lehr, Dr. Edwin E. *Colossus in Clay: Acme Brick Company, The Story of the Largest American-owned Brickmaker.* Virginia Beach, VA: The Donning Company Publishers, 1998. Pg. 7.
2. Ibid. Pg. 18.
3. Ibid. Pg. 19.
4. Ibid. Pg. 22.
5. Ibid. Pg. 23.
6. Ibid. Pg. 22.
7. Ibid. Pg. 25.
8. Bruner, Robert F. "The Financial Panic of 1907: Running from History." Smithsonian.com, 9 October 2008. http://www.smithsonianmag.com/history/the-financial-panic-of-1907-running-from-history-82176328/?no-ist=, accessed 7 October 2015.
9. Ibid.
10. Lehr, Dr. Edwin E. *Colossus in Clay: Acme Brick Company, The Story of the Largest American-owned Brickmaker.* Virginia Beach, VA: The Donning Company Publishers, 1998. Pg. 43.
11. Ibid. Pg. 45.
12. Ibid. Pg. 50.

Sidebar

1. Lehr, Dr. Edwin E. *Colossus in Clay: Acme Brick Company, The Story of the Largest American-owned Brickmaker.* Virginia Beach, VA: The Donning Company Publishers, 1998. Pg. 39.

Chapter 2

1. Lehr, Dr. Edwin E. *Colossus in Clay: Acme Brick Company, The Story of the Largest American-owned Brickmaker.* Virginia Beach, VA: The Donning Company Publishers, 1998. Pgs. 55–56.
2. Ibid. Pg. 58.
3. Ibid. Pg. 61.
4. Ibid. Pg. 64.
5. Ibid. Pg. 66.
6. Ibid. Pg. 66.
7. Ibid. Pg. 79.
8. Ibid. Pg. 75.
9. Ibid. Pg. 62.
10. Ibid. Pgs. 68–69.
11. Ibid. Pg. 63.
12. Ibid. Pg. 92.

Sidebar

1. Lehr, Dr. Edwin E. *Colossus in Clay: Acme Brick Company, The Story of the Largest American-owned Brickmaker.* Virginia Beach, VA: The Donning Company Publishers, 1998. Pg. 78.
2. Ibid. Pg. 84.

Chapter 3

1. Lehr, Dr. Edwin E. *Colossus in Clay: Acme Brick Company, The Story of the Largest American-owned Brickmaker.* Virginia Beach, VA: The Donning Company Publishers, 1998. Pg. 92.
2. Ibid. Pg. 99.
3. Ibid. Pg. 101.
4. Ibid. Pg. 97.
5. Ibid. Pg. 97.
6. Ibid. Pg. 105.
7. Ibid. Pg. 105.
8. Ibid. Pg. 114.
9. Ibid. Pg. 117.

Sidebar

1. Lehr, Dr. Edwin E. *Colossus in Clay: Acme Brick Company, The Story of the Largest American-owned Brickmaker.* Virginia Beach, VA: The Donning Company Publishers, 1998. Pg. 103.
2. Ibid. Pg. 105.

Chapter 4

1. *Company Annual Report*, 1959.
2. Lehr, Dr. Edwin E. *Colossus in Clay: Acme Brick Company, The Story of the Largest American-owned Brickmaker.* Virginia Beach, VA: The Donning Company Publishers, 1998. Pg. 122.
3. Robert A. Calvert, "TEXAS SINCE WORLD WAR II," *Handbook of Texas Online* (http://www.tshaonline.org/handbook/online/articles/npt02), accessed November 10, 2015. Uploaded on June 15, 2010. Published by the Texas State Historical Association.
4. Lehr, Dr. Edwin E. *Colossus in Clay: Acme Brick Company, The Story of the Largest American-owned Brickmaker.* Virginia Beach, VA: The Donning Company Publishers, 1998. Pg. 134.
5. Ibid. Pg. 134.
6. Ibid. Pg. 145.
7. Tomlin, D. O. "Letter to Acme Shareholders," 26 June 1968, Fort Worth marketing file.

Chapter 5

1. News Item, *Fort Worth Star-Telegram, November 22, 1968.* Pg. 1.
2. Ibid.
3. Farman, Irvin. *Standard of the West: The Justin Story* (Fort Worth: TCU Press, 1996). Pg. 173.
4. Ibid. Pg. 171.
5. Ibid.
6. Ibid.
7. Lehr, Dr. Edwin E. *Colossus in Clay: Acme Brick Company, The Story of the Largest American-owned Brickmaker.* Virginia Beach, VA: The Donning Company Publishers, 1998. Pg. 151.
8. Ibid. Pg. 152.
9. Farman, Irvin. *Standard of the West: The Justin Story* (Fort Worth: TCU Press, 1996). Pg. 180.
10. Ibid.
11. Ibid. Pg. 181.
12. Ibid.
13. Ed Stout Interview
14. Farman, Irvin. *Standard of the West: The Justin Story* (Fort Worth: TCU Press, 1996). Pg. 183.
15. Ibid.
16. Ibid.
17. Ibid. Pgs. 183–184.
18. Ibid. Pg. 183.
19. Ibid. Pg. 184.
20. Ibid. Pg. 185.
21. Ibid. Pg. 186.
22. Lehr, Dr. Edwin E. *Colossus in Clay: Acme Brick Company, The Story of the Largest American-owned Brickmaker.* Virginia Beach, VA: The Donning Company Publishers, 1998. Pg. 160.
23. Ibid. Pgs. 164–167.
24. Farman, Irvin. *Standard of the West: The Justin Story* (Fort Worth: TCU Press, 1996). Pg. 188.
25. Ibid. Pg. 189.
26. Lehr, Dr. Edwin E. *Colossus in Clay: Acme Brick Company, The Story of the Largest American-owned Brickmaker.* Virginia Beach, VA: The Donning Company Publishers, 1998. Pg. 171.
27. Ibid. Pg. 170.
28. Farman, Irvin. *Standard of the West: The Justin Story* (Fort Worth: TCU Press, 1996). Pg. 189.
29. Lehr, Dr. Edwin E. *Colossus in Clay: Acme Brick Company, The Story of the Largest American-owned Brickmaker.* Virginia Beach, VA: The Donning Company Publishers, 1998. Pg. 182.
30. Ibid. Pg. 261.
31. Author conversation with a high-school classmate, February 2015.
32. Harrold E. Melton, Interview Notes, Fort Worth, Texas, June 24, 2014; hereinafter referred to as Melton's Interview Notes.
33. Harrold Melton June 2014 Interview.
34. Ibid.
35. Lehr, Dr. Edwin E. *Colossus in Clay: Acme Brick Company, The Story of the Largest American-owned Brickmaker.* Virginia Beach, VA: The Donning Company Publishers, 1998. Pg. 264.

Sidebar

1. "Justin, H. J., And Sons," *Encyclopedia of the Great Plains,* http://plainshumanities.unl.edu/encyclopedia/doc/egp.ind.033
2. "John S. Justin Jr. Obituary," *Marietta (Oklahoma) Monitor,* March 2, 2001. Pg. 4
3. "Justin, H. J., And Sons," *Encyclopedia of the Great Plains,* http://plainshumanities.unl.edu/encyclopedia/doc/egp.ind.033
4. Ibid.
5. Lehr, Dr. Edwin E. *Colossus in Clay: Acme Brick Company, The Story of the Largest American-owned Brickmaker.* Virginia Beach, VA: The Donning Company Publishers, 1998. Pgs. 156–157.
6. Ibid.
7. Ibid. Pg. 157.
8. "John S. Justin Jr. Obituary," *Marietta (Oklahoma) Monitor,* March 2, 2001. Pg. 4.
9. Ibid.

Chapter 6

1. Lehr, Dr. Edwin E. *Colossus in Clay: Acme Brick Company, The Story of the Largest American-owned Brickmaker.* Virginia Beach, VA: The Donning Company Publishers, 1998. Pg. 232.
2. Ibid. Pg. 190.
3. Acme Brick Timeline.
4. Digitally Recorded Oral History Interview with Arthur Martinez, Jr., Fort Worth, Texas, February 17, 2015.
5. Ibid.
6. Ibid.
7. Ibid.
8. Lehr, Dr. Edwin E. *Colossus in Clay: Acme Brick Company, The Story of the Largest American-owned Brickmaker.* Virginia Beach, VA: The Donning Company Publishers, 1998. Pgs. 203–205.
9. Digitally Recorded Oral History Interview with Brent Snyder, Fort Worth, Texas, February 18, 2015.
10. Ibid.
11. Digitally Recorded Oral History Interview with Greg Hinnrichs, Fort Worth, Texas, February 19, 2015.
12. Digitally Recorded Oral History Interview with Mark Burden, Fort Worth, Texas, February 20, 2015.
13. Justin Industries, *1985 Annual Report.* Pg. 2.
14. Digitally Recorded Oral History Interview with Dennis Knautz, Acme Brick Company, Fort Worth, Texas, June 24, 2014.
15. Ibid.
16. Digitally Recorded Oral History Interview with Bill Lemond, Acme Brick Company, Fort Worth, Texas, February 17, 2015.
17. Ibid.
18. Ibid.
19. Digitally Recorded Oral History Interview with Susan Marvel, Acme Brick Company, Fort Worth, Texas, February 20, 2015.
20. Ibid.
21. Lehr, Dr. Edwin E. *Colossus in Clay: Acme Brick Company, The Story of the Largest American-owned Brickmaker.* Virginia Beach, VA: The Donning Company Publishers, 1998. Pg. 218.
22. Ibid. Pg. 236.
23. Digitally Recorded Oral History Interview with Bill Iiams, Acme Brick Company, Fort Worth, Texas, February 17, 2015.
24. Ibid.

Sidebar

1. Digitally Recorded oral history interview with Ed Stout, Fort Worth, Texas, June 24, 2014.
2. Ibid.
3. Ibid.
4. Ibid.
5. Ibid.
6. Ibid.

Chapter 7

1. Lehr, Dr. Edwin E. *Colossus in Clay: Acme Brick Company, The Story of the Largest American-owned Brickmaker.* Virginia Beach, VA: The Donning Company Publishers, 1998. Pg. 248.
2. Justin Industries, *1990 Annual Report.* Pg. 2.
3. Lehr, Dr. Edwin E. *Colossus in Clay: Acme Brick Company, The Story of the Largest American-owned Brickmaker.* Virginia Beach, VA: The Donning Company Publishers, 1998. Back Cover Flap.
4. Justin Industries, *1990 Annual Report.* Pg. 6.
5. Ibid. Pg. 19.
6. Ibid.
7. Ibid. Pg. 5.
8. Ibid.
9. Ibid.
10. Ibid. Pg. 2.
11. Lehr, Dr. Edwin E. *Colossus in Clay: Acme Brick Company, The Story of the Largest American-owned Brickmaker.* Virginia Beach, VA: The Donning Company Publishers, 1998. Pg. 243.
12. Ibid. Pg. 245.
13. Ibid. Pg. 246.
14. Justin Industries, *1991 Annual Report.* Pg. 2.
15. Ibid. Pg. 5.
16. Ibid.
17. Ibid. Pg. 6.
18. Ibid. Pg. 5.
19. Justin Industries, *1992 Annual Report.* Pg. 2.
20. Acme Brick Company, *Management's Discussion and Analysis of Financial Statements for the Month Ended December 31, 1992.* Pg. 1.
21. Ibid.
22. Ibid.
23. Ibid.
24. Ibid. Pg. 2.

25. Ibid.
26. Justin Industries, *1993 Annual Report*. Pg. 2.
27. Acme Brick Company, *Management's Discussion and Analysis of Financial Statements for the Month Ended December 31 1993*. Pg. 2.
28. Ibid.
29. Ibid. Pg. 2.
30. Ibid.
31. Justin Industries, *1993 Annual Report*. Pg. 2.
32. Justin Industries, *1994 Annual Report*. Pg. 5.
33. Ibid. Pg. 2.
34. Ibid. Pgs. 5–6.

Sidebar

1. Justin Industries, *1995 Annual Report*. Pg. 2.
2. "MR. BILL SEIDEL RECEIVES PRESIDENT'S AWARD FROM ACME BRICK COMPANY," Acme Brick Company Press Release, April 8, 2001.
3. Ibid.
4. Ibid.

Chapter 8

1. ACME BRICK CELEBRATES OPENING OF NEW PLANT NEAR SITE OF COMPANY'S ORIGINAL PLANT BUILT IN 1891, Acme Brick Company Press Release, November 6, 1996.
2. Ibid.
3. Ibid.
4. Justin Industries, *1996 Annual Report*. Pg. 5.
5. Ibid.
6. Ibid.
7. Ibid.
8. Ibid.
9. Acme Brick Company, *Management's Discussion and Analysis of Financial Statements for the Month Ended December 31, 1998*.
10. ACME BRICK ACHIEVES SALES OF ONE BILLION BRICK IN 1999, Acme Brick Company Press Release, February 16, 2000.
11. Ibid.
12. Ibid.
13. Acme Brick Company, *Management's Discussion and Analysis of Financial Statements for the Month Ended December 31, 1999*. Pg. 2.
14. "A Year of Positive Changes," *The Brick Press*, August 1999. Pg. 1.
15. EDWARD L. STOUT, JR., PRESIDENT OF ACME BRICK COMPANY, TO BE HONORED BY SALES & MARKETING EXECUTIVES OF FORT WORTH, Acme Brick Company Press Release, February 24, 1999.
16. Ibid.
17. Ibid.

Sidebar

1. Melton, Harrold E., "Interview Notes," June 24, 2014.
2. "Nomination of Harrold Melton for BIA Outstanding Achievement Award," Acme Brick Company, 2005.
3. Melton, Harrold E., "Interview Notes," June 24, 2014.
4. Ibid.
5. Ibid.
6. Ibid.
7. Ibid.
8. "Nomination of Harrold Melton for BIA Outstanding Achievement Award," Acme Brick Company, 2005.
9. Melton, Harrold E., "Interview Notes," June 24, 2014.
10. Ibid.

Chapter 9

1. Digitally Recorded Oral History Interview with David Michie, Fort Worth, Texas, February 20, 2015.
2. Ed Stout Interview.
3. Ibid.
4. "Acquisitions Increase Acme's Production Capacity," *The Brick Press*, August 1999. Pg. 2.
5. "Acme Brick Company Announces Acquisition of Wheeler Brick Company," Acme Brick Company Press Release, August 3, 2000.
6. "WARREN BUFFETT'S PURCHASE OF ACME BRICK A BONUS FOR HOMEBUILDERS," Acme Brick Company Press Release.
7. Harrold Melton Interview.
8. Ibid.
9. Ibid.
10. Ibid.
11. Digitally Recorded Oral History Interview with Dennis Knautz, Fort Worth, Texas, June 24, 2014.

12. Harrold Melton Interview.

13. Digitally Recorded Oral History Interview with Judy Hunter, Fort Worth, Texas, February 17, 2015.

14. Harrold Melton Interview.

15. Judy Hunter Interview.

16. "Warren Buffett's Purchase of Acme Brick a Bonus for Employees," *The Brick Press,* December 2000. Pg. 1.

17. "John Justin, 1917–2001," *The Brick Press,* April 2001. Pgs. 1–2.

18. "Acme Building Brands Acquires Holly Springs, MS Brick Plant," *The Brick Press,* July 2001. Pg. 1.

19. Ibid.

20. "Acme Buys Laufen Store and Warehouse," *The Brick Press,* July 2001. Pg. 1.

21. "Acme Purchases Denver Brick Co.," *The Brick Press,* December 2001. Pg. 1.

22. Ibid.

23. "Enterprise Resource Planning Underway," *The Brick Press,* December 2001. Pg. 1.

24. Digitally Recorded Oral History Interview with Rush Weston, Fort Worth, Texas, February 20, 2015.

25. Ibid.

26. Ibid.

27. Ibid.

28. Ibid.

29. Management Discussion, December 2004. Pgs. E-2, E-3.

30. "Harrold E. Melton Retires from Acme Brick; Dennis Knautz Becomes President & CEO," *The Brick Press,* April 2005. Pg. 1.

31. Ibid. Pg. 2.

32. "Robert L. (Bob) Stover Retires After 41 Year Career," *The Brick Press,* April 2005. Pg. 1.

33. "Stan McCarthy Named Vice President," *The Brick Press,* April 2005. Pg. 1.

34. "Bill Lemond Becomes Vice President," *The Brick Press,* April 2005. Pg. 1.

35. Dennis Knautz, "State of the Company: July 1, 2005," *The Brick Press,* July 2005. Pg. 1.

Sidebar

1. "America's Most Successful Investor Discovers Value of Acme Brick," Acme Brick Company Press Release, March 20, 2001.

2. Ibid.

3. "Melton Interview Notes," June 24, 2014.

4. Dennis Knautz Interview.

Chapter 10

1. Digitally Recorded Oral History with Harland Dixson, Fort Worth, Texas, February 9, 2015.

2. Ibid.

3. Ibid.

4. Dennis Knautz Interview.

5. "Happy 115th Berk-Day: April 17, 2006," *The Brick Press,* June/July 2006.

6. Dennis Knautz Interview.

7. Ibid.

8. Ibid.

9. "Letter from Dennis Knautz, CEO," *The Brick Press,* June/July 2007. Pg. 1.

10. Ibid.

11. Acme Brick Company, Management Discussion, December 31, 2007.

12. Ibid.

13. Acme Brick Company, Management Discussion, December 31, 2008.

14. Acme Brick Company, Management Discussion, December 31, 2009.

15. Dennis Knautz Interview.

16. "Elgin New Plant Completes Upgrades," *The Brick Press,* June/July 2007. Pg. 10.

17. "Ochs Brick & Stone Joins Acme Family," *The Brick Press,* March 2008. Pg. 1.

18. Digitally Recorded Oral History Interview with Joan Wylie, Fort Worth, Texas, February 19, 2015.

Sidebar

1. "Acme Brick Breaks Ground for New Fort Worth General Office on Oct. 6," *The Brick Press,* September/October 2006. Pg. 1.

2. "Acme Brick Headquarters," *MCAA Team Awards Winner,* http://www.masoncontractors.org/project/acme-brick-headquarters/

3. Ibid.

4. Ed Stout Interview.

Chapter 11

1. Bill Lemond Interview.

2. Ibid.

3. Ibid.

4. "From Dennis D. Knautz, CEO," *The Brick Press,* Fall/Winter 2011. Pg. 3.

5. Bill Lemond Interview.

6 "From Dennis D. Knautz, CEO," *The Brick Press,* Fall/Winter 2011. Pg. 3.

7. "Jenkins Associates Visit Fort Worth to Learn JD Edwards, *The Brick Press,* Fall/Winter 2011. Pg. 11.
8. "From Dennis D. Knautz, CEO," *The Brick Press,* Fall/Winter 2011. Pg. 11.
9. Ibid.
10. Ibid. Pg. 2.
11. Ibid. Pg. 3.
12. Ibid. Pg. 2.
13. "Management Discussion for the Month Ended December 31, 2013. Pg. 1.
14. Ibid. Pg. 3.
15. "Grand Openings for All 3 Patina Floor Design Stores," *The Brick Press,* Fall/Winter 2011. Pg. 1.
16. Stan McCarthy Interview.
17. Ibid.
18. "Management Discussion for the Month Ended December 31, 2013. Pg. 2.
19. Stan McCarthy Interview.
20. "Acme Brick Company Reopens Bennett, Texas Plant, Tuesday, February 5th In Response to Improving Homebuilding Market," Acme Brick Press Release, February 4, 2013. Pg. 1.

Sidebar
1. Dennis Knautz Interview.
2. Ibid.
3. Ibid.
4. Ibid.
5. Ibid.

Chapter 12
1. Dennis Knautz Interview.
2. "Dennis Knautz, President and CEO of Acme Brick Company Named Top CEO of a Public Company for 2015 by Fort Worth Business," Acme Brick Press Release, September 3, 2015.
3. Ibid.
4. Ibid.
5. Dennis Knautz Interview.
6. Ibid.
7. "Dennis Knautz, President and CEO of Acme Brick Company Named Top CEO of a Public Company for 2015 by Fort Worth Business," Acme Brick Press Release, September 3, 2015.
8. Dennis Knautz Interview.
9. Ibid.
10. Ibid.
11. Ibid.
12. Ibid.
13. Ibid.

Acme Brick Company memorialized its founding and early years in the 1890s and 1900s during its centennial celebration in 1991.

The centennial advertising campaign highlighted Acme Brick in the 1910s and 1920s.

In 1943, The Perla Plant Stopped Making Face Brick, and Only Made Products to Support The War Effort

The Bombing of Pearl Harbor on December 7, 1941, Brought The United States into World War II

Marines Raised The Colors in Victory on Iwo Jima in February 1945

In 1952, Acme Completed its Four Story Brick Office Building

America Launched its First Satellite ... Explorer I

King Size Brick Introduced

In 1960, Acme Purchased its First Mechanical Handling Equipment for Trucks

Franklin D. Roosevelt Inaugurated as President

As a Time When Two Thirds of The Nations Brick Plants Closed, Acme was able to Acquire The Bankrupt Bridgeport Plant and Survive The Great Depression

Tough Times, Soup Lines, and Nickel Apples

The Outbreak of World War II Signaled End of Depression

At its 1991 centennial, Acme Brick looked back on the 1930s, 1940s, and 1950s.

In 1991, Acme Brick created a centennial advertisement to celebrate the events of the 1960s.

The centennial celebration advertisement.

This 1991 centennial advertisement paid tribute to the 1970s.

INDEX

ABOUT THE AUTHOR

Writer and historian Bill Beck of Lakeside Writers' Group has more than a quarter-century of experience writing about business and institutional history. He wrote his first history for Minnesota Power in 1985, and has more than 130 published books to his credit. He has written anniversary books for Houston Lighting & Power Company and Central Power & Light Company in Corpus Christi. *Acme Brick Company: 125 Years Across Three Centuries* is one of his latest. He is currently completing an anniversary history for Donaldson Company in Bloomington, Minnesota.

Beck is a 1971 graduate of Marian University in Indianapolis and did his graduate work in American History at the University of North Dakota. Beck started Lakeside Writers' Group twenty-eight years ago following ten years as a reporter for newspapers in Minnesota and North Carolina and seven years as the senior writer in the Public Affairs Department at Minnesota Power, an electric utility in Duluth. He lives in the Irvington neighborhood of Indianapolis with Elizabeth, his wife of forty-nine years.